"*The Customer Experience Revolution* is a book that everyone who wants to succeed in business must read."

—Todd Robinson, Founder and Former Chairman, LPL Financial

"Companies that delight their customers outperform their peers. This guidebook tells us why and how they do it in industries as diverse as retailing, smartphones, food service and driver education. I highly recommended it to anyone building a customer-focused business or refocusing an existing business on the experience of the customer."

—Larry Tesler, Larry Tesler Consulting,
former Vice President and Chief Scientist, Apple Computer

"We've all heard about great companies like Starbucks, Apple, and Intuit, and we enjoy great experiences with them every day. However, few of us can truly articulate what it is that each of these experiences does for us, much less how we might replicate the experience in our own companies. *The Customer Experience Revolution* provides us with a great framework of understanding those experiences. It is a must-read for leaders who want to drive great customer experiences within their own organizations."

—Steve Albee, Senior Vice President, Union Bank

"Where does your brand begin and end? Where does your marketing stop and delivering online start? With cloud computing, online purchases, SAAS use, and live support in social forums, can you even define where your product experience begins and ends? These days you cannot and should not even try. Successful companies have prospered in response to these mega trends by taking the holistic approach described in *The Customer Experience Revolution* by Jeofrey Bean and Sean Van Tyne. This book is a must-read for anyone in the product delivery value chain. I fully recommend it."

—Daniel Rosenberg, SVP Product UX, SAP

"This is the best business book in years! Bean and Van Tyne do a brilliant job of analyzing what winners do to create a world-class customer experience. They spell out the winning steps so you can implement them in your business. If you want to increase sales and customer satisfaction and, at the same time, cut your costs, follow the advice in this book."

"Van Tyne and Bean explore case studies of some of today's most successful companies. As they look at their business, marketing and product design, it becomes clear that the secret to success is to put the entire organization behind creating an excellent customer experience at every point. The book is full of both cautionary tales and inspirational stories."

"*The Customer Experience Revolution* is a timely addition to any business reading list. This book provides insights to understand these changes and what companies of all sizes can do to embrace a successful customer experience strategy."

"*The Customer Experience Revolution* is a current and relevant book highlighting the key role customer experience should play in your company's business strategy. Extremely well-written in everyday language that we can all understand, Sean Van Tyne and Jeofrey Bean have thoughtfully made a case for the changing field of customer experience. Interspersed with high-profile case studies, along with practical advice, this book takes the reader from the beginnings of several start-up companies to their incredible success, and some to their very recent and untimely demise. This book is a must-read for the strategists in your company. If you don't think that your customer's experience with your company's processes, people, organization, and your brand are overwhelmingly crucial, think again. If you want to make your mark as a leader, engage your customers and act on the advice provided in this book."

"Across industries we're approaching the 'Vortex,' a feature horizon whereby winning customers and growing business is no longer a function of new features but something else entirely. Filled with accessible and thought-provoking examples, *The Customer Experience Revolution* demonstrates how organizations both large and small must engage with their customers to prevent commoditization and sustain a healthy bottom line."

—Darryl Kuhn, Chief Technology Officer, Skinit

"Creating an exceptional customer experience is critical to the long term success of business today. *The Customer Experience Revolution* contains a treasure trove of vignettes highlighting companies that really understand what it takes to improve customer relationships via a stellar experience. Gems and nuggets abound for the savvy business that wants to focus on their customers."

—Becky Carroll, Author of *The Hidden Power of Your Customers*, and President and Founder, Petra Consulting Group

"Every executive in most corporations will tell you how important it is to deliver the best customer experience. However, there are very few companies that do it in a repeatable way. Most corporations struggle and fail to make Experience Design an integral part of their company's culture. In *The Customer Experience Revolution*, Bean and Van Tyne have woven together essential concepts with real-world examples of what it takes to deliver awesome user experiences. In my view, this work will prove invaluable to people who need to make user experience an integral part of their business and their products."

—Ivan Crespo, Research & Design Software Engineering Manager, Eastman Kodak Co.

"Providing great customer experiences is the foundation of business success in the 21st century. In their new book, *The Customer Experience Revolution*, authors Jeofrey Bean and Sean Van Tyne show what separates great companies from also-rans, and what your company has to do today to join the revolution."

—Bilal Chinoy, Senior Vice President of Products, EMN8

THE CUSTOMER EXPERIENCE REVOLUTION

THE CUSTOMER EXPERIENCE REVOLUTION

How Companies Like Apple, Amazon, and Starbucks
Have Changed Business Forever

JEOFREY BEAN
SEAN VAN TYNE

BRIGANTINE MEDIA

Published by Brigantine Media
211 North Ave., St. Johnsbury, Vermont 05819

Cover and Book Design by Jacob L. Grant

ISBN 978-0-9826644-6-9

Other Brigantine Media books include:
Act Like You Mean Business by Rob Biesenbach
It's About Time by Harold C. Lloyd
The Big Picture: Essential Business Lessons from the Movies
by Kevin Coupe and Michael Sansolo
Am I The Leader I Need To Be? by Harold C. Lloyd
Business Success in Tough Times by Neil Raphel, Janis Raye, and
Adrienne Raphel
Win the Customer, NOT the Argument by Don Gallegos
Selling Rules! by Murray Raphel
Crowning the Customer by Feargal Quinn

For more information on these books please contact:
Brigantine Media
211 North Avenue, St. Johnsbury, Vermont 05819
Phone: 802-751-8802
Email: neil@brigantinemedia.com
Website: www.brigantinemedia.com

In memory of Steve Jobs 1955 - 2011
A visionary genius, inspirational experience maker,
and architect of the future.

Dedication

To Joanne and Laura
for their love and tremendous support
to make this book a reality.

Contents

Acknowledgements

THIS BOOK WOULD NOT HAVE BEEN POSSIBLE WITHOUT the support and encouragement from our family, friends, and colleagues. Most importantly, a very special thank you to Dr. David C. Gardner and Dr. Joely Gardner for their confidence in us and the insights and experiences they shared as authors of many published books. They generously gave their time and deep knowledge to mentor us through the book process.

We acknowledge the great Bill Gladstone, Kathleen Rushall, and all the helpful people at Waterside Productions. Two authors could not have asked for a better literary agency. This is true, too, for our publishers at Brigantine Media, Neil Raphel and Janis Raye. Neil and Janis have been a joy to work with—lots of laughs, exceptional ideas, and great conversations.

And we would like to acknowledge the very special professionals who directly shared their time, enthusiasm, and insights into how great companies create extraordinary experiences, and change industries and people's lives for the better. They are the heart and community of this book and include:

Bilal Chinoy
Senior Vice President of Products
EMN8

Ivan Crespo
R&D Software Engineering Manager
Eastman Kodak

Gari Garimella
Founder and Managing Partner
I DRIVE SAFELY

Kaaren Hanson
Vice President, Design Innovation
Intuit

Scott Jenson
Creative Director
Frog Design

Darryl Kuhn
Chief Technology Officer
Skinit

Pete Marlow
VP and General Manager, Corporate Communications and Marketing
J.D. Power and Associates

Donald Norman
Co-Founder and Principal
Nielsen Norman Group

Phil Ohme
Principal Interaction Designer
Intuit

Regina Pingitore, Ph.D.
Chief Research Officer
J.D. Power and Associates

Lisa Roth
CEO
Keystone Capital Corporation

Esther Stearns
President and COO
LPL Financial

Steve Swasey
Vice President, Corporate Communications
Netflix

Larry Tesler
Founder
Larry Tesler Consulting

Gary Tucker
Senior Vice President of Global Services and Emerging Industries
J.D. Power and Associates

Introduction
Customer Experience is the New Currency

*"We know from the data that people will pay
more for a better customer experience."*

—GARY TUCKER, J.D. POWER AND ASSOCIATES

THERE IS A SELECT GROUP OF EXTRAORDINARY COMPANIES that develop and deliver superior products and services. But they don't stop there.

These exceptional companies have shown us that great ideas and great products alone are not good enough. Not good enough for their customers and not good enough for their businesses or our future. These companies change people's lives, cause competitors to scramble to catch up, and transform their industries forever. These companies do it by purposely creating and delivering pleasing customer experiences. They delight people at every step of the customers' experience: intriguing them as potential customers, satisfying them when they become true customers, and continuing to outperform until their customers become advocates for their companies.

Some of these companies, like Amazon, Apple, and Starbucks, are household names. Other companies, such as

Intuit, are known mainly by their products (in Intuit's case, QuickBooks, TurboTax, and Quicken). Smaller, less well-known companies are customer experience leaders, too: Square, Skinit, EMN8, LPL Financial, and I DRIVE SAFELY. They are changing their markets and their customers' lives for the better. Large or small, famous or not, these companies are all part of the Customer Experience Revolution.

Few owners of the iPhone, drinkers of Starbucks lattes, or users of QuickBooks will tell you that they are customers because of price. They have become devoted customers because these companies and their products deliver an experience that they enjoy.

The companies that best understand the customer experience have an expansive vision of when that experience begins, and what that experience must be to convert prospects to customers to advocates. And they are committed to creating a great experience. They have surpassed ideas and technology. They have leapfrogged over products and services to deliver astonishing customer experiences.

CUSTOMER EXPERIENCE DEFINED

The customer experience is the sum total of all interactions a person has with a company. It starts when someone first interacts with the messages, people, or processes of a company's products or services. That interaction can be direct with the company's people or advertising messages. It includes the actual experience of directly making use of a product or service—what is known as the "user experience." Interactions that are part of the customer experience can also be indirect, through influencers such as reviews, articles, research, word-of-mouth, social networking, or from energized advocates of the company. All of these interactions, taken together, comprise the customer experience.

As of the writing of this book, we estimate that only about five percent of all organizations value and deliver exceptional customer experiences. But we predict that number will change, as companies learn the value added by great customer experience.

> **THE CUSTOMER EXPERIENCE is the SUM TOTAL of all INTERACTIONS a person has with a COMPANY.**

Gary Tucker is the Senior Vice President of Global Services and Emerging Industries for J.D. Power and Associates, a global marketing information firm that conducts independent research of customer experience, product quality, and buyer behavior. According to Tucker, "Delivering an extraordinary customer experience is becoming more and more important." Tucker says companies generally fall in one of three categories:

1. **Companies that really understand** the customer experience, and recognize its value as a competitive advantage.

2. **Companies that pay lip service** to the overall customer experience. They understand the concept, but aren't fully committed to it.

3. **Companies that just don't believe customer experience matters.** They don't think that customer experience is a place to differentiate. Such companies tend to be in more commodity-driven businesses.

Tucker says the old concept of customer satisfaction is too narrow. Satisfaction is the difference between what a customer expects and what a customer gets. It is still an important ingredient, but customer commitment is a much more effective measure of experience. Says Tucker, "The outcome is customer *commitment*, not satisfaction." Measuring a customers' level of commitment is to gauge what J.D. Power calls "stickiness," or the "propensity to buy a product or service again."

SETTING THE BAR

Gina Pingitore, J.D. Power's Chief Research Officer, says, "When you have a company that sets the new bar on expectations, it sets the bar for every company." She cites an example: "Amazon fundamentally changed the way that people interact and expect to interact with all online providers. Amazon remembers what you bought, suggests what you might like, but doesn't oversell. It is a very easy point-and-click experience that sets the new stage for people's expectations across many industries. They start to think: 'Why can't I book a hotel as easily as I can buy from Amazon? Why can't I do other things that easily?' Companies that innovate a better customer experience and successfully deliver it ultimately set the bar for *all* companies."

Most customers do not categorize and compare their experiences by industry. They enjoy a customer experience that one company provides, and they begin to expect that same experience from other businesses. Therefore, it is critical for companies to go outside of their industry to benchmark the best experience companies. Tucker says, "The next frontier is not *within* an industry, it is *outside* the industry, benchmarking the leading practices as consumers experience them. As a customer, I don't benchmark my experience with Hilton Hotels exclusively with my experience with the Four Seasons." Smart companies should use such companies as Apple, Starbucks, and Amazon as role models for customer experience, no matter what the industry.

MEASURING CUSTOMER EXPERIENCE

New ways of defining and measuring the value of customer experience are emerging. J.D. Power issued a report in February 2011, "Achieving Excellence in Customer Service," that measured customer interaction with the J.D. Power 5 Ps^{SM}: a company's *people, presentation, price, product,* and *process.* They are the drivers of excellence for customer experience.

J.D. Power measured the J.D. Power 5 Ps^{SM} in its analysis of feedback from hundreds of thousands of U.S. consumers who do business with more than 1200 different companies. After looking across dozens of industries, they identified forty companies that stood out from the rest, delivering an experience consistently superior to their competition. They called these companies "J.D. Power Customer Service Champions."

The data shows that these forty companies share one extremely significant attribute. They do more than *deliver* on their customers' expectations—they *exceed* them. In doing so, they raise people's expectations for their competition.

Some examples of how companies exceed customers' expectations include:

- Employees who are encouraged and empowered to help solve customers' problems. (Ritz-Carlton and Four Seasons Hotels)

- Products enhanced through effective packaging and merchandising effort. (Caribou Coffee)

- Prices that reflect value. (Wegman's Pharmacy, Lincoln and Cadillac automobiles, and Quicken Loans)

- Easy, effective, and fast interactions. (Amazon's and Zappos' product delivery and return policies)

BETTER CUSTOMER EXPERIENCE BRINGS BETTER REVENUE

According to J.D. Power's Tucker, "We know from the data that people will pay more for a better customer experience." One example from J.D. Power's research involved wireless telecommunications providers, typically one of the toughest categories from a customer experience standpoint. A study examined service scores for wireless telecommunications providers from syndicated analysis in 2008 and 2010. They were then compared with the publicly-available financials of these wireless telecommunications companies, such as net subscriber additions (i.e., the number of new customers minus the number of lost customers) and operating revenue.

Overall, J.D. Power's analysis showed a positive relationship between the customer experience of wireless telecommunications providers and their financial results. This relationship held over time (i.e., two-, three-, and four-quarter lags), but was strongest after the first quarter. The differences among these three groups are statistically significant and lead to dramatic differences in financial performance. Failure to excel in the minds of customers can have far-reaching implications to a company's bottom line.

This principle works for a small company on a limited budget as well as a large institution. A company can calculate how much money it will spend to make a positive difference for its customers. Then the company can make the return on investment linkage specific to its prospects and customers. Finally, it can measure the improvements investments in experience have made in customer attitude toward the company and its market share.

J.D. Power's Pingitore offers some advice to those at companies who want to improve on their customer experience. She says, "First, consider where you are on the customer experience continuum:

- "If you are a company that is way below par on delivering the customer experience, then you probably want to benchmark yourself against people that are mediocre in your industry. Get the basics right.

- "If you are at par, then you need to begin benchmarking yourself against companies that are the best in class and usually deliver more than just the basics.

- "If you are a company that is one of the best in your industry, start looking at similar or even dissimilar industries to figure out what lessons and innovations can be learned to help you think beyond what you are currently doing."

Forrester Research, a market analysis company that focuses on technology firms, has its own customer experience index that is updated and reported annually. This work was pioneered by Bruce Temkin, whose report, "The State of the Customer Experience, 2010," concluded that 90 percent of North American companies with revenues of $500 million or more view customer experience as critical or very important to their company's strategy. Temkin also noted that 80 percent of companies want to use customer experience as a form of differentiation.

Forrester's customer experience research has shown a high correlation between customer experience and three vital types of customer behavior:

1. Willingness to buy more
2. Reluctance to switch
3. Likelihood to recommend

For large companies, a small investment in customer experience does positively affect the bottom line. Forrester looked at $10 billion companies across 12 industries and found that for those companies that successfully focused on customer experience, average annual revenue increased by $284 million.

Forrester also looked at the percentage of devoted customers within the customer bases of more than 100 companies. They found that customer experience leaders have an advantage of more than 14 percentage points over customer experience laggards across all three indicators of consumer behavior. In the service industry, the study found that the annual revenue gains from a modest improvement in customer experience could total $311 million for a large hotel. Banks and hotels garnered the largest gains from their current customers, while airlines gained the most from customers who advocate for them. Customer experience improvements boost revenue.

WALL STREET REWARDS CX

John Picoult of Watermark Consulting examined whether the stock market recognized the value of companies with superior customer experience in his study, "Is the Market Rewarding Customer Experience Leaders?" Picoult carried out an analysis of stock market performance for groups of customer experience leaders and laggards from Forrester's research from 2007 through 2009. The top ten and bottom ten publicly-traded companies from Forrester's rankings were selected. A comparison was then made between the total returns from investing in an equally-weighted portfolio of customer experience leaders to that of customer experience laggards and the broader market of companies included in the Standard & Poor's 500 index.

Picoult found that the customer experience leader portfolio outperformed the overall stock market. The top ten customer experience leaders generated cumulative total returns that were 41 percent better than the S&P 500 Index. Further, the customer experience leaders' combined returns were 145 percent better than the group of companies that were customer experience laggards. The results were consistent in each of the three years, with the customer experience leader portfolio always outperforming the group of companies that were customer experience laggards.

Since the years 2007 through 2009 were turbulent years for stock market values, it is interesting to see how the customer experience leaders held up relative to the broader market. The value of the customer experience leaders group did indeed decline with the rest of the market during the recession. However, their decline was significantly less pronounced than it was for the broader market and even more so for experience laggards. As the force of the economic recession weakened in 2009, the customer experience leaders portfolio had more than doubled the return of the S&P 500 by year-end.

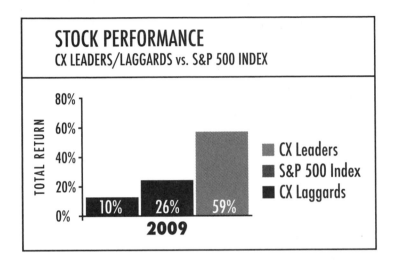

Research analyst Andrew McInnes, working for Forrester Research, tested Picoult's method and results, and confirmed Picoult's findings: "The customer experience leaders consistently outperformed the other two groups; the customer experience laggards consistently fell short."

The results of the research by these professionals help to confirm the importance of developing and delivering extraordinary customer experiences. Such independent confirmation shows that the customer experience revolution is the new way for companies to compete and excel, especially during tough economic times.

CUSTOMER EXPERIENCE HAS GREAT VALUE

The research results, along with the performance of companies like Apple, Starbucks, Amazon, and Intuit, have shown us that the value of extraordinary customer experiences is a powerful and effective currency. Once people have an extraordinary experience with a company, they value it above other alternatives available to them. Companies have opportunities to be the first to change the currency of their markets, by positively transforming the experience continuum. Once this happens, as it has in the smartphone, home video, personal finance, and video camera markets, among others, those markets are permanently transformed. Competitors in a market who do not improve their customer experience will be trading with a less valuable currency going forward. They may be trading on price or features or another currency that can be devalued by a competitor's superior customer experience.

Avoiding the vortex

A market for a new product is made of customers with similar needs. Those customers will pay higher prices for products and services when they like the innovative ideas behind them.

However, high prices and high profit margins will not last. Economic, technological, or competitive factors will one day cause a company's profit margins to sink. The success of the attributes that make products more valuable breeds competitors and imitators. In time, these valuable attributes are found in many other products. Customers will pay less because the product has lost its distinguishing characteristics and value.

At that point, the company that makes the product has a challenge. It needs to find a way to renew the product so it is once again different, better, and more valuable than what is now commonly available.

Many companies choose only to keep adding more features and more capabilities, and often the time between these renewals gets shorter and the upgrades more expensive. Even when companies find a way to add features cheaply, there are other risks to consider. People may stop responding if they do not see value in the next round of features or new capabilities. Eventually, people become fatigued with additional features. At this point, a company may have unknowingly entered the Vortex.

The Vortex is the strong current in a market that demands that competitors add more features and capabilities while profit margins shrink. The Vortex is efficient at making commodities of anything it can pull in. The strong current of the Vortex demands that changes in products or services occur more often and in smaller time periods. The distinctions between competitors' products in the minds of customers are rapidly erased along with the participating companies' profitability. Frequently, companies see no other way to compete and preserve value than to out-feature the competition. They may call it an "upgrade," but often the profits from the product go everywhere *except* up.

> THE VORTEX
> is the strong current
> in a MARKET that
> # DEMANDS
> that competitors
> ADD MORE FEATURES
> and CAPABILITIES
> while
> profit margins
> SHRINK.

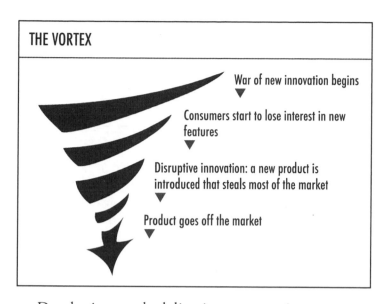

THE VORTEX

War of new innovation begins

Consumers start to lose interest in new features

Disruptive innovation: a new product is introduced that steals most of the market

Product goes off the market

Developing and delivering a superior customer experience is a key way for a company to stay out of the Vortex. In their 1999 book, *The Experience Economy: Work Is Theater & Every Business a Stage*, B. Joseph Pine II and James H. Gilmore predicted the importance of customer experience to today's economy: "In an age of commoditization where most products and services are undifferentiated, consumers shift their focus from product and service attributes to the experience obtained while using the product or service. The more relevant and memorable the experience, the higher the value, the higher the worth, the higher the price that can be charged." When a product becomes commoditized, re-thinking the customer experience with the product will be far more valuable for retaining and building new customers than adding expensive new features.

In an interview with the *San Diego Union-Tribune* in January 2011, Michael Capone, marketing professor at San Diego State University, commented on the need to compete using customer experience rather than price:

"Cutting prices is not sustainable differentiation, but creating new and exciting shopping experiences can create a strong consumer preference."

EXAMINE THE DO-FORS

To avoid the Vortex, companies must understand their Do-Fors. The Do-Fors are what products or services *actually do* for customers that they *highly value*. They answer the questions: *What will that do for me?* and *Why should I care?* Delivering them well with an extraordinary customer experience can create advocates and additional revenue.

A close examination of a product's Do-Fors will reduce guesswork and help keep a company from adding unnecessary and expensive features. Knowing what the customers want and how they want it gives a company the  information it requires to determine and develop an experience that pleases the customer.

Getting the Do-Fors right is no accident. It takes research, observation, and product trials to learn what the Do-Fors are. And they can change as technology changes or competitors develop something new. But building a customer experience around the Do-Fors is a great way to ensure success.

CUSTOMER EXPERIENCE IS CRUCIAL

Potential and existing customers are having experiences with a company's people, processes, products, or services regardless of whether or not the company is purposely creating those experiences. The customer experience starts long before people are customers. The experience begins when

> The **DO-FORS** are what **PRODUCTS OR SERVICES** actually **DO** for customers that they **HIGHLY VALUE.** They answer the questions: *WHAT WILL THAT DO FOR ME?* **and** *WHY SHOULD I CARE?*

people come in contact with a company's messages, people, processes, products, or technology, directly or indirectly. In the world of social media, experiences can come secondhand from other people, processes, technology, or messages. The totality of customer's experiences with a company is now a key determinate of a company's success or failure.

Customer experience influences people's intent to purchase and their willingness to pay. Customer experience influences actual and perceived ease of use of a product. And customer experience influences consumers' actual and perceived value of a service. Customer experience influences people's happiness and the rate that they will convert from customers to enthusiastic advocates for the company.

Businesses now have to deliver an exceptional customer experience. This customer experience includes every aspect of the business relationship with the customer:

- the promises in the first ad or review that someone sees;
- the way a company's website projects the product or service;

- what a Facebook friend has to say about his or her experience;

- how a company representative responds on the phone;

- how easy it is to make a purchase or a return;

- how the product comes through with the promises that have been made

The companies that best understand the value of the customer experience deliver a consistent, pleasurable, and valuable experience from the first time a person interacts with a company, to the receipt and use of the product or service, and throughout the customer's relationship with the company.

LEADERS OF THE CUSTOMER EXPERIENCE REVOLUTION

To fully understand the impact of the customer experience revolution, it is important to look at some of the companies that have created a tremendous advantage by developing and delivering the best customer experiences. This book will tell the stories of some very well-known companies, including Apple, Amazon, Intuit, Mini Cooper, Starbucks, and Netflix. The book also includes stories of less well-known companies, including LPL Financial, Skinit, EMN8, I DRIVE SAFELY, and Square. All of these stories demonstrate how superior customer experience helped the companies achieve success. Through their examples, we will draw principles that any company in any industry can use to become a customer experience leader.

This is a revolution that every company must join in the next decade. Companies can learn from the profiles in this book, and use the principles to create great experiences for their customers to gain a significant competitive advantage.

In the words of Amazon CEO Jeff Bezos (as quoted by Joe Nocera in the *New York Times* in January 2008): "The reason I'm so obsessed with these drivers of the customer experience is that I believe that the success we have had over the past twelve years has been driven exclusively by that customer experience."

The customer experience revolution has begun.

Chapter 1
Time for a Revolution

"We're going to put a ding in the universe."

—STEVE JOBS

T HE CROWD AT THE MACWORLD EXPO IN SAN FRANCISCO on January 9, 2007 could barely contain its excitement.
For months, rumors had been circulating that Apple Computer was going to roll out a blockbuster product, a product as significant as the 2001 introduction of the iPod. A confident Steve Jobs entered the stage, peered out at the suddenly hushed crowd, and confidently announced, "Today, we are going to reinvent the phone." It was a brand new phone from a company new to the phone market.

Apple launched the iPhone. And in a few short months, the phone industry was changed forever.

It was a bold step. Apple was entering a field crowded with tough and experienced competitors. Where exactly was the opportunity for a new entrant to compete with all those successful companies making phones? Some companies already in the market manufactured phones with great value. And others were adept at consistently introducing new technologies, styles, and advanced features.

Before 2007, there were already many successful companies making smartphones, which combine computing, Internet connectivity, and other capabilities into a wireless phone. Before Apple entered the market, these smartphone companies included formidable competitors such as Nokia, Research in Motion's BlackBerry, Motorola, and Palm. These telecommunication giants leapfrogged each other every three months, constantly adding innovative features and functions.

> ...SUCCESS wasn't about THE TECHNOLOGY, FEATURES, THE CALLING PLAN, or the price. Apple iPhone DELIVERED EXACTLY WHAT IT PROMISED —an EXTRAORDINARY experience.

Suddenly, one day, with one announcement, Apple changed the playing field by changing customers' expectations of what a smartphone should do for them. In the first year of production, Apple sold 3.7 million iPhones, with one million sales in the two months following its introduction.

Before the iPhone, Apple was primarily a computer company, not a phone manufacturing company. And its entry into the phone market was in many ways a competitive failure. The iPhone was expensive, with a poor camera, no 3G capabilities (a standard at that time), no keypad, and no memory card. In addition, it could be obtained from only one wireless service provider, AT&T,

and required a two-year contractual commitment to be linked to its wireless network. But this technologically weak and feature-poor product transformed customers to enthusiastic advocates at a rate unseen in the smartphone market.

As Apple saw it, success in this market wasn't about the technology, features, the calling plan, or the price. While all those are important ingredients, Apple's iPhone delivered exactly what it promised—an extraordinary *experience*. From the time people heard about the iPhone until they became customers and then enthusiastic advocates, the iPhone offered, by far, the best smartphone experience.

Customers flocked en masse to phone stores to replace their old phones with the new iPhones. Even though their old phones were quite adequate, they wanted the charm, buzz, coolness, fun, aesthetics, and prestige of Apple's new product. Most of all, they wanted what they heard so much about from other iPhone owners—the pleasurable experience of using it. This was something unavailable from any other phone in 2007.

Best of all for Apple shareholders, the iPhone was extremely profitable. Apple grossed 50 percent on each sale, gained 14 percent of the cell phone market in a year, and its stock rose 44 percent. The industry and its customers were so changed that four years would pass before another company, as new to the phone industry as Apple was in 2007, would directly challenge the iPhone.

That company was Google, which introduced its Android phone in January 2011. And the people at Google are every bit as passionate and committed to anticipating, creating, and coming through with remarkable customer experiences as Apple. Like Apple, Google has superior brand and technical staff that continue to innovate faster and better than most of the competition.

It is no accident that in the experience revolution, these two players, new to the phone industry, are battling for smartphone supremacy. They are both masters of customer experience—changing industries and customers' lives forever.

CREATING THE IPHONE CUSTOMER EXPERIENCE

The iPhone offered an innovative experience by intimately understanding and anticipating what people wanted to do with their smartphones and what experience they wanted doing it. Apple carefully combined technology from other products into a hand-held device to purposely create a pleasurable experience for the smartphone user. The iPhone promised and delivered that pleasurable experience as a phone, an Internet communicator, and a music player.

Apple began studying the market and the competitors at least three years before the introduction of the iPhone. The best customer experiences had come from easy-to-use *QWERTY* keyboards, phones that were smaller and lighter than average phones, built-in cameras, Bluetooth compatibility, and screens that made it easier to make and receive calls.

The phone makers often included a stylus to poke and type on the tiny keys of their phones. The stylus was generally unpopular. It was an enlarged toothpick-like pointer, a potentially dangerous poker that was precarious to use. People would worry about where the stylus was or even lose it. The real job of the stylus was to help people adapt to the phone maker's hardware. The stylus got in the way. When smartphone owners were focusing on poking their device, the stylus ultimately disconnected most of them from the world around them.

Phone makers promised ease of use. But customers'

actual experiences were hampered by phones that had cramped keyboards and tiny hardware pieces that many reviewers and users experienced as feeling like plastic toys. Broken promises, hardware-centered experiences, and a decline in consumer confidence in existing smartphones created an opportunity for Apple to create a better product.

The smartphone experience Apple created started with the elegance of the phone itself. During the iPhone introduction in January 2007, Steve Jobs confidently asserted that Apple designed something that fits beautifully in the palm of your hand. Most people agreed. The iPhone was thin—at 11.6 mm in depth, thinner than any smartphone ever before. It had a 3.5-inch high-resolution screen that occupied most of the iPhone's front. This touch screen was accompanied by only one button in the center below it. That button took you "home." Having only one button made it difficult to get lost.

Apple changed everything by drawing on insight about what makes successful interactions between people and computers. They replaced the user-resistant fixed-in-plastic buttons and tiny keyboards with a daring interface. The stylus was replaced with the human finger—what Jobs called, "The best pointing device in the world. One we are born with." To assure that the screen and finger were a gratifying and efficient combination, Apple developed what it calls "Multi-Touch" for the screen. Multi-Touch fine-tunes the screen to interact with people's fingers by ignoring unintended touches and hover motions. Kiosks had used touch-screen technology for years, but Apple was the first to bring a refined version of touch-screen technology to the phone. In addition, the iPhone let you "pinch" the screen with your thumb and forefinger to zoom in and out on a Web page, map, or photo.

This intuitive touching of the screen, or gesture-based interface, allowed users to "flick" through a menu, between photos, or from one screen to the next. This is very much like the experience of turning the pages of a book in real life. It is natural, engaging, and for many, fun. Gesture-based interfaces are not new, but Apple made them new on a phone. A blog post by the *New York Times* columnist David Pogue quoted a customer who said, "It's fast, beautiful, menu-free, and dead simple to operate." Another customer commented in an online iPhone review, "I honestly can't describe to you how much of a pleasure the iPhone is to use, and compared to pretty much any other mobile device, it's in a completely different league."

Jobs spoke out passionately during the iPhone's introduction, saying, "most phones have software that is crippled." He promised that the iPhone would now give us "real desktop-class applications at least five years ahead of the software that is now on any phone." It did. And it did it with software that supported almost everything that people wanted to do with phones and computers in 2007, including high quality sound, animation, networking abilities, power management, and security.

E-mail was fully formatted, including graphics. You could open Word, Excel, and PDF documents. Within only three years of its introduction, the iPhone offered a selection of over 300,000 applications including games, lifestyle, social networking, and education apps.

The lure of the iPhone confounded many competitors. Some of them had trouble understanding the customer experience advantage of the iPhone. In an interview with *Bloomberg Businessweek*, former Nokia manager Dave Grannan described how Nokia management viewed the new competition. When the iPhone was announced, "it was widely disregarded. The attitude was that we'd tried touch screens before, and people didn't like them. [The iPhone] had no multimedia messaging capability. The reception and sound quality were poor. It couldn't be used with one hand. There was nothing to fear."

Inside Nokia, there was no curiosity about why the iPhone was suddenly so successful. There was no meaningful review of what changed the context of the market and created new customer expectations. Nokia's legacy company mind-set was still evident three years later. In 2010, Stephen Elop became Nokia's new President and CEO. His mission: to turn the company around. A story in *Bloomberg Businessweek* recounts an early meeting with employees. Elop noted a problem with too many different keystrokes needed to mark an e-mail unread on different Nokia phones. A Nokia engineer said Elop was wrong, so Elop asked him to demonstrate otherwise. The engineer tapped on a phone for a while, then was forced to admit that Elop was correct. Nokia's share of the smartphone market has gone from 49 percent before the introduction of the iPhone to 25 percent as of the first quarter of 2011.

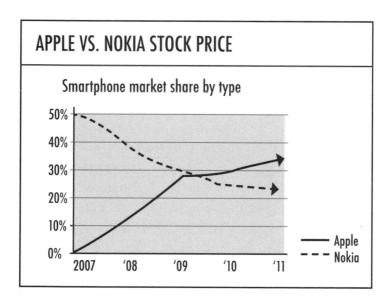

APPLE VS. NOKIA STOCK PRICE

Smartphone market share by type

The introduction of the iPhone is just one of an unprecedented series of product successes Apple has had in the last decade. The iPod, iPad, and various operating system and computer hardware improvements have all made Apple a company that customers care about. Apple's ability to give customers a great "Apple experience" has made that company a formidable competitor.

Apple is committed to being in the business of delivering extraordinary experiences and generates sustainable value from its investment in that area. Morningstar, Inc. points out in its analysis of Apple in the smartphone market in early 2010, "We believe Apple's soup-to-nuts model of integrated hardware, software, and application distribution is the key to the iPhone's success because it allows Apple complete control over the user experience. The elegance of the iPhone's user experience has attracted a multitude of users with more than 33 million units shipped to date. The growth in users has in turn brought software developers to the platform, and most importantly, developers are making money selling applications in the App Store."

The same can be said of Apple's success creating the market for the tablet with the iPad. With an average selling price of $595 to $645, the iPad sold almost 15 million units worldwide in 2010 since its introduction in April of that year. Apple purposely created the tablet market by developing and delivering positive customer experiences for mobile customers. With the release of Apple's operating system Lion, the customer experience on the computer now matches the mobile experience, with touch-screen capabilities that customers have come to expect across all Apple's products.

The iPhone is a great example of how a company can create a complete customer experience that results in major success. Apple did its homework before it entered the smartphone market, and then designed the product from the ground up to reflect how customers would want to use it. The iPhone included the features that were important to customers—Internet connectivity, phone and texting, a music player, strong graphics for games—and paired them with an ease-of-use sensibility that no other smartphone offered. Apple has been a leader in design aesthetics since its inception, and the iPhone continued that tradition with its minimalist look that is driven by the way the product works.

All of these factors taken together make the customer experience of the iPhone one that is exemplary, and one that keeps customers buying every time a new iPhone is introduced.

Customer experience is key to success today. A thoughtful, well-designed customer experience will take a product from good to great, and will make a company a market leader. Apple has used customer experience to capture new markets that have turned the company from a quirky computer manufacturer to a technology powerhouse.

Chapter 2
Customers Take Charge

"We lived in farms, then we lived in cities, and now we're gonna live on the Internet!"

—SEAN PARKER, *THE SOCIAL NETWORK*

LISTEN TO YOUR CUSTOMERS. THAT'S ADVICE EVERY marketing consultant gives to every client. But too few companies really know *how* to listen—and how to *respond* so that customers will pay attention. What is the best way for a company to solicit input from customers?

The popularity of websites such as Yelp or TripAdvisor or Angie's List shows an ever-growing reliance on online review information written by customers, not experts. Companies that understand the importance of the customer experience know how to use social media to get customers to comment, then listen to what their customers have to say, and incorporate those ideas into the customer experience.

Customers are also becoming the drivers of the platform on which a company offers its products or services. How many of us choose the ATM over the teller line at the bank, or the self-scanner at the supermarket to avoid the longer checkout lanes? Customers are choosing what kind of experience they want to have, and when. (Are you reading this book as a physical book, on a tablet or e-reader, or are you listening to it?) The best companies know how to expand their reach to customers with social networking and communications devices to deliver exceptional experiences to all their customers—in any and every way the customer chooses to get the experience.

STARBUCKS—WOULD YOU LIKE SOME FEEDBACK WITH YOUR LATTE?

Starbucks was in trouble. Huge trouble.

For fifteen consecutive years, the upscale coffee seller Starbucks had top line growth of at least 20 percent each year. But in 2008, the company suddenly lost over 50 percent of its operating income and its operating margins. The great recession put a damper on the number of customers ordering a Starbucks double-tall-one-pump-vanilla-skim-caramel macchiato. The economic times were changing and Starbucks was losing momentum.

Most of the stores that were underperforming had been recently opened. Starbucks' priorities were to increase its market share in existing markets, primarily by opening additional stores, and to open stores in new markets. This strategy stopped working as the overheated national economy slowed down. The high growth rate of new stores was threatening Starbucks' long-time commitment to delivering a consistently positive and engaging customer experience.

By September 2008 the U.S. economy was plummeting at high speed with no end in sight. The financial and real estate institutions that the country depended on were failing at an increasingly accelerated rate. Starbucks' stock reached an all-time low of $7.83 a share in November

2008, a continuation of a steep value slide from $38.41 on October 6, 2006. Of its 9,000 stores worldwide, the company committed to closing approximately 600 under-performing company-operated stores in the U.S. and 61 stores in Australia.

It was time for a new direction. Howard Schultz had built the company but had stepped down as CEO for several years. He came back with enthusiasm and new ideas, and revitalized a failing company by improving the company's customer experience.

Starbucks was a leader in customer experience from its start. In 1982, Howard Schultz worked for Starbucks at Pike Place Market in Seattle as the director of marketing for the coffee bean retailer. Schultz's inspiration for Starbucks cafes came from a trip to Milan, Italy, where he noticed that the small cafes that dominated most street corners were an important part of people's everyday lives. Schultz saw that people were not just at the cafes for a high-quality cup of coffee. They were there to connect with other people while having coffee in a comfortable, casual place. He returned to Starbucks with the idea of recreating that kind of customer experience in the U.S. Schultz left Starbucks to start his own cafe in downtown Seattle called Il Giornale, named after a local newspaper in Milan. It was a shop that not only served great coffee, but also offered its customers the "third place" experience he had enjoyed in Milan—not home, not the office, but a new destination to meet people and enjoy conversation.

In 1987, with the backing of local investors, Schultz bought Starbucks and launched the first significant geographic expansion of the Starbucks experience.

The business continued to succeed and expand, opening cafes around the globe.

By the end of 2000, Starbucks had more than 3,500

> With the
> CONCENTRATION ON GROWTH
> and the RELEVANCY
> of its
> CUSTOMER EXPERIENCE
> in DECLINE,
> STARBUCKS had
> ENTERED THE VORTEX
> of COMMODITIZATION

locations worldwide, serving more than 12 million customers per week in 17 countries, with revenues that reached $2.2 billion for the year. The cafes tailored the customer experience to the locales. The 2002 Annual Report summarized the way Starbucks fine-tuned the customer experience: "As we reached out to more customers than ever, we thought you might like to know how we're delivering the experience in Spain. In Madrid, we open early and close late. A citrus juicing machine presses sweet *naranjas*, glass by glass, and the most popular breakfast is a traditional sticky *caracola de chocolate* and a *caffè latte*."

The next year, Starbucks gave customers in-store high-speed wireless Internet access, responding to the new way customers were "connecting" at Starbucks.

Next, Starbucks used music to invigorate the customer experience. In 2004, the company opened a Hear Music™ Coffeehouse in Santa Monica, California. Based on the acquisition of a music catalog company and later agreements with recording labels, the Hear Music brand became the music played in each store, including in-store sales of standard and exclusive music, branded retail stores, and a label to distribute recordings. As of 2005, Starbucks reached 10,500 stores around the world.

By 2007, though, something was wrong. Inside Starbucks there was worry.

2007 was the first year that customer traffic at Starbucks in the U.S. declined. The number of Starbucks stores continued to grow—now to 15,011, a 17 percent increase in 12 months. Net revenues grew to $9.4 billion, and passed the expected 20 percent mark by 1 percentage point. But important indicators of sustainability were pointing down. Operating income was up by 15 percent, but the margins from it were slightly down, for the second consecutive year. Same store sales were down for the third year in a row, to 5 percent in 2007.

ENTERING THE VORTEX

With the concentration on growth and the relevancy of its customer experience in decline, Starbucks entered the Vortex of commoditization—that strong current in a market that demands that competitors give more and lower prices while profit margins shrink. The Vortex makes commodities of anything it can pull in. In his autobiography *Onward: How Starbucks Fought for Its Life without Losing Its Soul*, Schultz acknowledged that in its tremendous growth period, Starbucks made decisions that "led to the watering down of the Starbucks experience, and what some might call the commoditization of our brand."

Schultz understood what had been lost at Starbucks: its extraordinary customer experience. He and his team set about determining how to reinvigorate that experience. The biggest challenge facing Schultz was how to make Starbucks more relevant and exciting to customers. The critical pieces to the turnaround included: dramatic cost reductions and process improvements, better beverages from innovation and better training, value offerings and loyalty programs, improved customer service, and tastier and healthier food.

But there was another enormous influence for customers that was changing the way customers "shopped, purchased, and communicated about products and services," according to a special report by J.D. Power and Associates. Customers were communicating via social media, and the voice from this channel was loud and unavoidable.

Schultz knew firsthand from Michael Dell himself about the issues Dell Computer had dealt with in 2005 and 2006. Jeff Jarvis, a dissatisfied Dell customer with an influential blog, used his clout in the online world to get the attention of the founder and CEO of Dell Computer. Dell eventually recognized the need to not only respond to Jarvis, but to create an online presence where customers could solicit ideas from customers, based on their needs. Dell's experiment with social media was hailed within the company as a success, and Schultz recognized the value of a proactive approach with customers to help build Starbucks' customer experience.

MyStarbucksIdea.com

Starbucks decided to embrace the changing nature of its customer base. Salesforce.com helped Starbucks develop MyStarbucksIdea.com, a social networking community of Starbucks customers. The site actively solicits ideas from customers and allows people to vote for the best ones. The ideas are sorted by categories: products, experience, and involvement.

According to Matthew Guiste, Starbucks' Global Social Media Director, the new social technology platform includes a live feed of everything posted to its sites, including customer ideas and the actions taken by Starbucks. The site shows ideas that have been implemented and also ideas that have not been accepted. Guiste believes it is important to show customers the reasoning behind its decision to accept or reject an idea.

Within a few months after its start, the site generated tens of thousands of ideas from Starbucks customers. MyStarbucksIdea.com has a fresh look and feel. It is easy to find what you are looking for and has friendly, familiar icons and graphics.

As of the end of May 2011, over 250,000 people have signed up, and 109,000 ideas have been posted, garnering over one million votes.

Starbucks recognized the value of using social media as a two-way communication channel, rather than a one-way method of delivering marketing messages. According to Guiste, "It's about relationships, not marketing. We consciously did not want to have 12 Facebook pages and 15 Twitter accounts, each for a specific department. We intentionally want there to be one place to start with us in each channel. Any new community we launch is always '/Starbucks'."

MyStarbucksIdea.com has been very successful at initiating profitable marketing ideas that further the customer experience. Customers initiated the idea that became Starbuck's Treat Receipt, giving customers discounts for a cold beverage in the afternoon after making a purchase in the morning. Starbucks first tested the idea in several cities and then launched the program nationally. Afternoon sales increased. Customers also made it clear that the Starbucks rewards loyalty program was important to them, so in late 2009, Starbucks integrated its Reward and Gold Cards into a single new program, My Starbucks Rewards. In about one year, according to Schultz's autobiography *Onward*, more than $1.5 billion had been loaded onto My Starbucks Rewards cards.

In a video presentation, Guiste offered these insights about what success looks like for a new social media site:

- It gives your fans great content.
- How many fans or followers you have doesn't matter—its what they do that counts.
- Visitors can read or watch something that makes them feel good about the company.
- There are positive responses. You can vote or comment on ideas.
- Customers can sign up for further communication.
- People can share content of the site with someone else.
- Buying something is not the primary driver for content.
- Customers become advocates for the company. But being a Starbucks fan is not a requirement for commenting.

PEOPLE WILL TALK

Although some management personnel at Starbucks were leery of this new site, such discussions were already taking place. Many people had already established their own unofficial Starbucks websites. An unofficial blog called "Starbucks Gossip" already contained postings such as news releases, articles, and anonymous opinion pieces.

People will have customer experiences with your company, its messages, products, or services, regardless of whether you are in charge of them. Starbucks, like Dell, had other blogs commenting on the company. Without an official Starbucks-hosted interactive website, independent sites become the default hosts of important two-way exchanges about a company's people, processes, products, or services.

Few companies have the resources to respond to all ideas, comments, and concerns posted by customers in real time. But customers want real-time responsiveness. Starbucks' site resolved this dilemma with an innovative solution. Forty monitors from Starbucks interact live with customers on the site, each for at least two hours a week. The monitors are food or beverage developers, community strategists, or quality managers. People vote on the posts with a thumbs-up. The ideas that get the most points and conversation are the ones that the monitors respond to. According to Chris Bruzzo, VP of Brand, Content, and Online for Starbucks, in a presentation he gave in 2010 at the Social Good Summit, having experts listening to customers helped Starbucks truly understand the power of bringing customers into the conversation.

MyStarbucksIdea.com was the first step to connect with customers outside the stores. The company next added Facebook and Twitter to their social networking mix. Today, the company uses Twitter mostly as a way to understand customer reaction to Starbucks. The company sometimes sends out tweets, but more often, Starbucks follows other Twitter posts to see how people are reacting to its products and services. According to Guiste, Starbucks has two or three people that follow Twitter posts on their screen all the time.

RESULTS

Starbucks began to reap the benefits of its social media efforts in 2009. The company's 2009 Annual Report notes that, "Because of this renewed customer focus, the company's customer satisfaction scores increased a full 10 percentage points." The new offers and loyalty card program based on the ideas from MyStarbucksIdea.com were instrumental in helping Starbucks revitalize the customer experience and, in turn, the company's profitability.

While new revenues were off compared to 2008, the big sign that the turnaround was beginning was in operating income and margins during 2009. Operating income increased six percent over 2008. The downward slide of operating margins stopped for the first time in four years.

Howard Schultz noted that 2009 was the year the company stopped trying to protect what it had and, instead, became proactive in dealing with its customers' new ways of communication.

During 2010 Starbucks revenues increased to a record $10.7 billion. Operating income increased to $1.4 billion, an $857 million increase in just one year. Starbucks earned an operating margin of 13.3 percent in 2010. This was the second consecutive year of margin growth and the highest operating margins Starbucks had ever reached. The company offered its first-ever dividend for shareholders and partners. Starbucks was as solid as any company could be amidst a continuing economic downturn.

In the Starbucks 2010 Annual Report, Schultz confidently asserted that the company's operational foundation and a heightened level of innovation and customer relevance had repositioned Starbucks to not only grow, but also to leverage earlier and new-found strengths inside and outside the stores. The company started multi-brand product development (Including VIA® Ready Brew, Tazo® and Seattle's Best Coffee®) and introduced a digital network to bring customers news and entertainment. Schultz acknowledged the vital contribution of MyStarbucksIdea.com and external social platforms in determining and delivering the revitalized customer experience and business results. The Annual Report noted that Starbucks was one of the top brands on Facebook.

A report by Morningstar in April 2011 commented on Starbucks overall market position after the turnaround and diversification into retail and consumer goods. "With café-like environments and a brand that invokes a high-quality customer experience, Starbucks enjoys pricing power advantages over these specialty coffee peers, in our view."

The outlook for Starbucks is now very good. Revenues are expected to grow in the mid-to-high single digits. Same store sales are expected to show mid-single-digits while the company expands internationally by 500 stores, including 100 in the U.S. Operating margins will likely stay the same or improve somewhat.

In *Onward*, Schultz looks back at the turnaround and revitalization of Starbucks in a short time and sums it up this way: "There are companies that operate huge global networks of retail stores, like us. Others distribute their products on grocery store shelves all over the world, like us. And a few do an extraordinary job of building emotional connections with their customers as we have learned to do. But only Starbucks does all three at scale, and we increasingly see a future where each complements the others, forming a virtuous cycle that allows us to go to market and grow the company in a unique way."

THE CUSTOMER IS IN CHARGE

Customers are taking charge in the customer experience revolution. People are now communicating with new platforms such as smartphones, tablets such as the iPad, and are interacting more extensively with companies through such social media networks as Facebook and Twitter, as well as newer ones like Google+.

J.D. Power's research notes this shift in the way customers want to communicate with companies. In its February 2011 report on Achieving Excellence in Customer Service, J.D. Power says, "Benchmark companies have learned that customers want to engage with a product or service provider in a place, at a time, and through a communication channel of their own choosing."

Starbucks initially engaged social media platforms as part of its turnaround. The company recognized the need for something to jumpstart the conversation with its customers, and used social media platforms to engage that discussion. Starbucks showed its customers that it had a commitment to use the information they received from customers, letting Starbucks customers know that they are important to the company's growth.

SOCIAL MEDIA—LIKE RUNNING WATER

Businesses need to know what platforms their prospects, customers, and advocates use. They also need to know what platforms are coming in the future that people will likely embrace. The wireless network cloud is here to stay. Just as running water, electricity, and automobiles innovated new lifestyles and economies, the wireless cloud is doing the same. And like running water, electricity, and cars, those who are born and come of age with it do not know life without the cloud.

You don't want to be separated from potential customers and existing customers because the preferred communications platform changed. Businesses that use new platforms to create exceptional customer experiences will be the businesses that thrive in the future.

REVOLUTIONIZING THE SELF-SERVICE EXPERIENCE

One company that has energized the kiosk platform is EMN8, a manufacturer of self-service ordering kiosks for fast-food restaurants. EMN8 has done so by focusing on the customer experience while in the restaurant and while using the kiosk.

EMN8 knows their Do-Fors for their customers—the restaurants:

- Increase the average check
- Improve the speed of service
- Lower transaction costs

In order to satisfy the Do-Fors, EMN8 wants to create what they call "an easy, fast and engaging experience" for the restaurants' customers, by creating multi-lingual automated ordering kiosks.

EMN8 was founded in 2002 and has approximately sixty employees. Growth rate for worldwide unit sales in 2011 is at one hundred percent. EMN8 was selected for the North America 100 and the Global 100 Red Herring lists of the most promising private technology ventures in North America. EMN8 crafts the customer experience of using the kiosks at Quick Service Restaurants (QSR) and fast casual dining restaurants, which include

Jack-In-The-Box, Burger King, Domino's, and Carl's Junior (with annual revenues of $2.9, $8.6, $3.3, and $1.3 billion, respectively).

Bilal Chinoy, Senior Vice President of Products at EMN8, discussed why EMN8 has succeeded at the self-service kiosk where others have failed. "There were other attempts to do self service in the fast food industry and casual food markets, but it never succeeded, for a number of reasons. One of them is the whole user experience. What we did was revolutionize that. Rather than take a very computer-driven approach, we decided our role was to guide the user experience. We focused on the user instead of the computer."

EMN8's kiosks create a more immersive customer experience when ordering and selecting food, streamlining the self-service process by guiding the customer through the selection of choices. EMN8 introduced "suggestive sell options," which resulted in increased spending by each customer and more revenue for the restaurants. Using these, the average spend by a customer placing a self-service order increased ten to thirty percent. Chinoy said, "Delighting the customer is a really big influencer, before and during the selection, then at the point of purchase."

The EMN8 kiosk experience delights the customer by replacing the counter experience, which can be fraught with human error. The kiosk is an alternative to the long lines at the counter—especially important since people are hungry. Many people do not like the experience at the counter when ordering. EMN8's research and development data and actual sales results show that younger customers, in particular, actually prefer an automated process, because they are in control of their own order. Accuracy is increased with the order by kiosk, so there are fewer surprises in the bag or on the tray. The kiosks also can help overcome language issues, because several different language options are available on the kiosk. This assists in speeding orders.

Chinoy described a strikingly counter-intuitive finding about personal interactions that was uncovered during the product's development. "A *minority* of people likes human interaction," said Chinoy. "The majority doesn't think automation is a cold way of doing business. For most people, particularly young people under 35, human interaction is not important."

CUSTOMER COMMUNICATION PLATFORMS

The communications platforms for generating and keeping business can be:

- analog—live presentations, speaking and personal calls

  or

- digital—email, websites, video, smart-phones or tablets

It is imperative to understand which platforms are important to prospects and customers, both in current use and what may be adopted in the near future. Customers will often use a combination or a portfolio of platforms.

While technology companies may create new platforms, people choose which ones they will use. People choose which new ones pass from fads to part of day-to-day life. Communications platforms can be used for promotions, building customer connections, transactions, actual delivery of the product, or many other reasons. Regardless of what the platform is supposed to do, the experience people have with the platform can be decisive in converting a prospect to a customer and a customer to an advocate.

Discovering the Do-Fors

At the core of the customer experience that people will have with a communications platform are the Do-Fors— what products or services actually *do for* them that they highly value. Do-Fors are more impactful than tag lines, and more important than lists of features and specifications. Do-Fors answer the questions: *What will that do for me?* and *Why should I care?* The Do-Fors for EMN8's ordering kiosks for casual dining restaurants are: Increase average check and improve speed of service at a lower cost. Creating a great customer experience requires real knowledge of the markets, the potential customers, and the context of the competition. Having valuable Do-Fors is not an accident. Do-Fors are an important part of the process for creating a great customer experience.

What the Customers Really Want

The company ComplianceMAX used the concept of Do-Fors to help build the business. Like many companies, ComplianceMAX had avoided real understanding of what its customers wanted. Instead, the company tried to sell more, sell harder, lower prices, and add

Having valuable DO-FORS is not an ACCIDENT. DO-FORS are an IMPORTANT PART of the process for CREATING the GREAT CUSTOMER EXPERIENCE.

more features. When that all failed to bring the results the company sought, ComplianceMAX eventually proceeded to find out exactly what those Do-Fors were.

ComplianceMAX started in 2003 with the goal of helping its clients stay in compliance with complex, ever-changing, legally binding financial regulations. ComplianceMAX's chief salesperson was co-founder Lisa Roth, a financial compliance expert, who travelled around the country speaking and selling ComplianceMAX software and consulting services directly to small- and medium-sized companies. Additionally, the company sold at conferences and to industry contacts and people in their professional networks. While the company had a respectable client base, by the end of year two, growth had slowed. There was concern about the future.

Roth recalled the situation of the company at this critical juncture: "We were very much a startup company for what felt like too long. We wanted to expand and we wanted to scale." The company engaged a consultant to help with the process. Roth said, "The consultant asked if we knew exactly what we did for our clients. We stumbled around and none of us could really articulate it."

The consultant recommended that they listen to what ComplianceMAX's prospects and customers said about what the company does for them that is better and different from the competition. That information would be instrumental for determining how to present the company and connect with the market.

Roth said, "We thought that it just can't be that easy. If it was that easy, I could just call my clients and find out."

The ComplianceMAX team focused on selling more and selling harder. But the growth problem still shadowed them.

Roth and her team returned to the consultant's

recommendation that they had dismissed as overly simplistic. According to Roth, "We started making phone calls to our clients." The phone calls proved to be eye-opening.

Clients were not interested in talking about compliance. They were, in fact, completely confident that ComplianceMAX was taking care of their regulatory requirements. Repeatedly, clients said, "I don't worry about compliance because I know you have me covered." This was a defining moment of change for ComplianceMAX.

"In the beginning, we thought that our value proposition was our ability to scale and stay on top of rules and drill down technologies," said Roth. "We realized that wasn't it at all. Our value proposition was our ability to translate all of that into plain English." ComplianceMAX's slogan had been "Our People and Our Technology." ComplianceMAX drove its revenues that way, built its office that way, hired people and used technology that way. "When we were done really listening to our prospects and customers," said Roth, "We added one line to our original value proposition and it then became, 'Our People, Our Technology, Your Peace of Mind.' It worked and was the perfect evolution."

The company used this new information to transform the ComplianceMAX website. Instead of expanding it to include lots of rules and tout their experience, ComplianceMAX cut out almost all the hard information. "We took the bullet points off our website," said Roth. "We put up green grass and blue sky and a few pictures of people. We showed them our personality. We showed them that we weren't compliance geeks."

It was the beginning of getting the company on a sustainable growth path. Roth said, "After we formulated our message and began marketing in earnest, our numbers soared. We went from a company of 100 clients to a company of 1,000 clients in 18 months. We enjoyed profitability within 24 months."

The company found that having the "your peace of mind" message on their website expanded the company's reach to a whole new community of firms, including brokerages that had broad distribution to many broker/dealers. Instead of going to small independent companies one at a time, ComplianceMAX could go to brokerage firms, each serving many brokers, or to their broker/dealers and appeal to them.

Growth came quickly. ComplianceMAX was founded in 2003, and in August 2007, with its base of 2000 broker-dealer and investment adviser clients, ComplianceMAX was acquired by National Regulatory Services.

ComplianceMAX used one of the oldest analog communications platforms—telephone calls—to ask their customers about what was important to them. Then they used a more modern digital platform—their website—to communicate back to the customers about the benefits of ComplianceMAX to generate huge company growth. They succeeded because they communicated well on the platforms their customers were comfortable using.

Chapter 3
Ask, Watch, and Listen

"To understand the man, you must first walk in his moccasin."

—NORTH AMERICAN INDIAN PROVERB

WHEN BETTY CROCKER INTRODUCED ITS FIRST CAKE mix in 1947, the company was sure it would be an instant success. Instead of spending hours making a cake from scratch, housewives only had to open the package of Betty Crocker cake mix, add water, and bake. Sounded like a winner. But customers rejected the product. Betty Crocker's parent company, General Mills, was perplexed: Why didn't busy housewives want to use the cake mix?

After spending some time talking to customers, General Mills figured it out—the mix made cake-baking *too* simple. There was no "pride of ownership" in the cakes baked with the mix. They tasted fine, but they weren't "homemade." Part of the pleasure of presenting a homemade cake to your family was the knowledge that you had done it yourself, and stirring mix and water together was clearly not enough.

The solution: General Mills modified the Betty Crocker cake mix recipe to require the addition of an egg. Sales of the cake mix soared.

Knowing your customers is a necessity for building a great customer experience. According to Gina Pingitore, J.D. Power's Chief Research Officer, companies today need to "Ask the customers and watch what they do through different activities...we call it 'Ask, Watch, and Listen.'"

When building an exceptional customer experience, the customer controls the conversation and the company needs to be a good listener.

A TEDIOUS JOB SPARKS A NEW COMPANY

Personal computers were still a novelty in 1982. IBM introduced its PC only the previous year, and people were wondering what, besides spreadsheets and word processing, could be done with them. Noting people's frustrations with balancing the checkbook and paying the bills, it occurred to Scott Cook that bill payment—writing checks and reconciling balances—was a chore a computer could do with ease.

In 1983, Cook co-founded Intuit to create Quicken, the personal finance software that overwhelmingly dominates its market today.

He named the company "Intuit" because he wanted its products to be so easy to use that customers would intuitively know how to do it. And he named its first program "Quicken," meaning both "to speed up" and "to give life."

FOLLOW YOUR CUSTOMERS

When Intuit first introduced Quicken, there were a handful of competitors, most of whom had more features than Quicken. Quicken took over the market, in large part because Scott Cook spent hours watching his customers balance their checkbooks and pay their bills. He didn't release Quicken until he knew that his customers could quickly and easily do their most important tasks.

Today, Intuit still asks, watches, and listens to customers. Intuit calls these site visits "Follow-Me." They will follow their customers at a restaurant and watch them while they are using their mobile devices. They will follow them in their cars, or follow them while they are in their offices. Kaaren Hanson, Vice President of Design Innovation at Intuit, explains the idea behind the Follow-Me method. "More than just following them where they use the product, [we] follow them *where they are living their lives.* That might give you insight as to where else that product might be useful or where else you might be able to solve their problem. It can give you a lot of information and inspiration."

> When you are **OBSERVING** don't just LOOK AT WHAT YOU CAN FIX— look for where you **CAN** make your EXPERIENCES exceptional.

Phil Ohme, Principal Interaction Designer at Intuit, says that when you follow a customer, you must "get outside your comfort zone. Figure out what is going wrong and where the opportunities exist to do things better. When you are observing, look at what can take it up a notch. Don't just look at what you can fix—look for where you can make your experiences *exceptional.*"

During "Follow-Me" sessions, Ohme has found that

customers sometimes create their own solutions to problems they find when working with Intuit's products. A customer may have created special "cheat sheets" for information that they need to use the product or service—sticky notes all over the place or a spreadsheet on the computer to manage information—that could be incorporated into your solution and completely change their interaction with your experience. "If a customer has a 'work-around' and it gets them to where they are going faster, get that into your solution because it is probably going to work for everybody," says Ohme.

DO IT EARLY, DO IT OFTEN

Intuit learned to use this strategy of observing customers during product development after the company experienced some unsuccessful product launches. Ohme notes that, "At Intuit, it used to be called 'launch and learn.' We had some really bad launches and failures. Now we have more soft launches, where you launch it to a small group of users and see how it goes. Then you go to 100 customers, and see where that goes. And you constantly make the product better. Then you go to 1,000. Then you make it available to the public.

Intuit involves customers and potential customers as early as possible and as often as possible in the product design process. The company recognizes that getting customer input in the early stages saves time and money later, when it is harder and more time-consuming to make course corrections or rework the product. Many companies prefer to "launch and learn," but they run the risk of learning that they have lost customers, prospects, market share, and revenue, by involving customers too late in the process.

Netflix uses a similar strategy of following customers

to observe how they interact with the product. Steve Swasey, Vice President of Corporate Communications at Netflix, says, "We go to people's homes and sit with them while they watch a movie and we watch what they do. Do they go to the remote control? Do they go to a cable channel? Do they put a DVD in the tray?" Netflix has a special center at their headquarters with a big "living room" with televisions and laptops, where company observers can watch customers behind a two-way mirror. "We tell participants, 'Here are three versions of a new user interface,'" said Swasey. "They use them and we watch how many times they click on the mouse, we watch their eyeballs and how they interact."

Gary Tucker, Senior Vice President at J.D. Power and Associates, says that companies need continuous customer feedback built into their processes. "Delighting your customers is not a destination, because when you get there, what it takes to delight them just got harder or changed. Improving and delighting is a constant evolution."

Intuit's "Follow-Me-Home" program is that company's way to get regular customer feedback, so the customer experience is always being refreshed and improved.

CUSTOMER INFORMATION THROUGH PROFILES

Skinit, a company that personalizes the exterior of various consumer devices, also enlists customers for information about its products. Skinit's technology lets consumers personalize their electronic gadgets with an image—their favorite sports team, college, Disney character, film, video game, or their own creation. Skinit's first product, the "skin," is a pressure-sensitive adhesive that consumers apply onto devices like cell phones, laptops, tablets, MP3 players, and gaming consoles. People "skin" their devices to show their style or support their favorite team.

In 2006, Skinit had ten employees making personalized adhesive logos and other artwork for consumers to stick onto electronic devices. The personalization trend for consumer electronics was just beginning to pick up and there were only a few small players in the market. Skinit made the decision early on to focus on quality. Skinit needed to establish a large brand library, and to do that, they had to ensure the brands that they could be comfortable entrusting them with their content and name. Because the market was so nascent, getting brands to sign up was difficult. In most cases, the consumer electronics category hadn't been licensed to anyone else. By focusing on quality, Skinit offered security for well-known companies. Their brands wouldn't be compromised if they worked with Skinit.

Skinit secured more brands than any other offering. Brands recognize that personalization offers a way to build affinity with their base and evangelize their brand externally. As consumer electronic devices are increasingly becoming less differentiated from competitors, manufacturers are looking for an edge. Offering personalization helps to sell the product. In addition to offering products under its own brand name, Skinit also has "white-label" and "enterprise" offerings running personalization campaigns for companies like Microsoft, Verizon, Sprint, and AT&T.

Skinit is now the global leader in "consumer electronic device personalization" and powers numerous personalization programs for *Fortune* 1000 companies, including the medical, wireless, retail, consumer electronic, home appliance, and commercial graphics markets. The Skinit platform can be offered as a complete turn-key software and service solution, or as a stand-alone hosted software solution. Skinit drives a multitude of proprietary and open source manufacturing technologies such as laser etching, paint on-demand, digital print, film conversion, and many others.

BUILDING THE SKINIT CUSTOMER EXPERIENCE

In 2007, Skinit was preparing to introduce the "Customizer" to enhance its previously successful Photo Uploader, a web-based application that allows consumers to upload their own photos and manipulate designs for their personal electronic devices. The objective was to provide an intuitive and flexible interface with a rich customer experience that increased conversion.

In order to understand what that customer experience should be, Skinit's Chief Technology Officer, Darryl Kuhn, created customer profiles for each group of customers who use Skinit's products. Building the profiles began with examining analytic data gathered from Skinit's website, then third-party demographic and psychographic (lifestyle) information data was added to complete the picture.

Customers who look at certain kinds of skin designs typically fall within a certain profile. Kuhn gives examples of the way customer profiles work: "Using analytics and demographics we gather from our online offerings, we can see that older populations skew toward more patriotic themes. We know sports skew to certain regions of the country. We know that certain brands skew to younger audiences."

Using these profiles, Skinit can make connections between the various themes that customers purchase and recommend products that will be meaningful to them. The profiles also help to identify customers who will buy more than one item at a time.

Skinit used these profiles to great advantage in the redesign of the Customizer. Kuhn explains the early design process: "First we tested the Customizer with the employees here at Skinit. We chose people who were new to the company or hadn't ever used the Customizer." Soliciting employees was easier, faster, and cheaper than finding and bringing in people from outside. Then Skinit recruited friends and family who met the target profile—another quick and easy way to get the feedback they needed to move the designs along.

Kuhn began to understand that rather than trying to assume that he knew what was in the mind of the customer, he needed to review the designs with customers to be sure the content was clear. The answers would let him know if the customer was having a good experience with the product and what changes needed to be made.

The process of showing customers prototypes of new products convinced Skinit of the value of being test- and data-driven. Says Kuhn, "You have to learn to give up the ego and be willing to live with the results. The alternative is to continue to interject your own ideas—guesses—and continue to design experiences that your customers don't understand or like or want. "

By integrating knowledge of their customers' goals into their redesign process, Skinit delivered a solution that exceeded projected revenue estimates. They produced a customer experience that increased conversion by 350 percent. According to Skinit co-founder Darrin Hegemier, "Having a more compelling customer experience met the immediate goal of increased conversion and revenue from our Customizer application, but perhaps more significantly, it placed us in a clear leadership position in the personalization space, meeting our long-term strategic objectives as well."

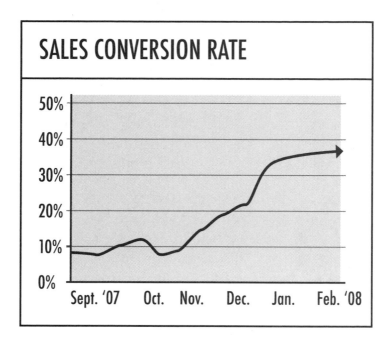

SALES CONVERSION RATE

THE WHAT AND THE WHY

Getting customer data through both observation and analytic tracking is a valuable combination for developing the best customer experience. Intuit's Kaaren Hanson explains, "Analytical data will track people from the offering through various sites and that will tell you what they are doing when they are in the space. But the observational data lets you know what they are doing when they are not being tracked. Observation gives you insight. There are certain times of the day when you are using your phone or computer. There is a lot of stuff that is happening around your use of the device. If we were simply tracking the data and analytics, we would not get that. Both qualitative data and quantitative data can be very useful for inspiration."

Analytics can tell you the "what," but talking with and observing your customer will tell you the "why." You can then test new ideas with customers to see if they solve the issues you have uncovered.

YOU ARE NOT YOUR CUSTOMER

Scott Jenson has worked with top customer experience companies such as Apple and Google. Jenson says, "The biggest surprises almost always come in user testing, when I've taken my precious little baby and I put it in front of users. There are times when the users just have no idea what's going on, and they're hopelessly lost. What really separates good designers from everybody else is the number of mistakes that they've made." Jenson recognizes that a good customer experience designer knows that he or she *doesn't* know and has the humility to figure it out and make lots of mistakes until it's right.

Larry Tesler was Vice President of Shopping Experience at Amazon and notes an example of the value of customer input. Amazon was running a super saver shipping program, but customers were having difficulty finding the information. Teslar says, "Customers were hunting all over the page to find out whether the product qualified for super saver shipping—the message was an inch away from the price, but they didn't see it. Jason Kilar, a product executive, asked us to test a tiny revision to one sentence: 'Change the word *and* to an ampersand.'" Tesler didn't think a change that trivial would make any difference, but to placate Jason, he agreed to give it a try. They ran tests with customers, and the ampersand change worked. Being creative and testing with customers helped Tesler remember: you are not your customer. "Just because it doesn't make sense to you doesn't mean it won't make perfect sense to your customers," says Tesler.

Ask your customers what they want; *watch* them interact with your solutions; and *listen* to what they say.

Chapter 4
Less Can Be More

"We're not going to add features and functions"

—Jonathan Kaplan, CEO, Flip Video

THE BEST CUSTOMER EXPERIENCE DOES NOT ALWAYS mean complexity. A great customer experience can result from selective editing. Think about the Google home page—a masterpiece of simplicity.

The Flip video camera was a highly successful example of judicious editing for the improvement of the customer experience. The camera was intentionally designed to leave out a number of features and functionality currently available in other video cameras. The Flip was designed for a fun experience, and it more than delivered on its promise.

The roots of the Flip were in another product, a single-use digital still camera from little-known Pure Digital Technologies, a small company with less than 100 employees. That camera was available in 2001 at most pharmacies under a myriad of brands for about $20. It was designed to be returned to the drugstore so prints and picture CDs could be created for customers. Pure Digital Technologies needed those cameras to be returned, to save money when they reused the shells of the returned cameras to manufacture new cameras.

But many of the cameras were never returned. The savings needed from reusing shells of returned cameras fell short. Pure Digital Technologies could no longer continue in business with the digital cameras, even though they were still selling. Where did they go? What were people doing with them?

It turned out that many customers were hacking into the cameras. After they were opened, people would connect them to a computer and upload the photos onto the Internet. It was easy to do with a disposable camera, and people were eager to upload photos to share with their friends via the Internet. Those hackers would unknowingly play an important role a few years later in redefining video cameras.

The founders of Pure Digital Technologies, Jonathan Kaplan and Ariel Braunstein, had failed with their idea of the single-use digital still camera. So they turned their attention to video cameras.

In the stagnant, thirty-year-old video camcorder market, Kaplan and Braunstein saw only high-end, complicated products. The market was cluttered with cameras using a wide variety of recording formats. The most affordable camcorders sold for $350-$500, and prices skyrocketed from there, depending on the additional components needed for optimal results.

The cameras came in a variety of shapes. The standard shape was a camera you held like a football. The upright model was held like a soda can. Larger camcorders needed to be perched on a user's shoulder. It was necessary to bring along blank videocassette tapes, DVDs, or memory cards when you wanted to film, not to mention lens caps and batteries. When you wanted to watch a video, you needed the camera, along with connecting cables, tapes, and a screen on which to view. For many customers, using the camcorder was a bigger event than what they were filming—so the cameras weren't used.

Kaplan and Braunstein understood that adding more features was not what customers wanted. The camcorder market needed a point-and-shoot video camera.

Based on their experience with hackers using their disposable still photo cameras, they developed a new digital video camera that could easily connect to a computer and the Internet. As with still photos, customers were interested in recording videos quickly and immediately sharing them on the Internet, via YouTube and other sites. The new video camera was designed around what customers wanted it to do—its Do-Fors.

The Flip's Do-Fors: To record, connect, and share videos.

From the start, Kaplan was committed to delivering a customer experience designed around the Do-Fors of recording, connecting, and sharing that would be *fun*. Part of building the fun customer experience involved the product name. When the product entered the market in 2006, it was called "Pure Digital PSV-351 30 Minute Point-and-Shoot Camcorder." The product took off when the name was changed to the "Flip" in 2007. According to Kaplan in an interview with Kara Swisher of All Things Digital, the "Flip" name came from the concept of the car key that flips out from the holder when you press a button.

On the Flip, the USB arm flips out from the top of the camera with the push of a button. The Flip gets plugged right into the computer, becoming a place for storage and transfer, familiar and easy to access by the user. This feature virtually guaranteed that there was little for customers to learn before starting to share their videos.

The Flip required no special accessories, software, cables, or other components. Kaplan was happy *not* to include those extras, along with the other things customers did not want. Since the Flip was essentially a camera plus computer drive, customers no longer had to carry around spares of blank videocassettes, DVDs, or memory cards.

The Flip Ultra video camera measured only about four by two inches. It was thinner than one inch at its deepest point and only had a few buttons to operate the camera below the small one-inch screen on its back.

This first version made low-quality, 640 x 480 resolution video. The competition from Sony, Canon, and others offered cameras that nearly doubled that video sharpness and clarity. This, along with the lack of obvious features on the Flip confounded many reviewers who were used to comparing camera features, fineness of video resolution, and price. Some reviewers never considered fun, ease of use, or customer experience as part of the Flip's benefits.

As planned and promised to customers, users of the Flip needed only a few minutes to record, connect to the Internet, and begin sharing their videos. An early Flip Ultra package promised the Flip owner "easy video uploads to AOL, Myspace.com and YouTube!" The Flip delivered. It was a perfect complement to the fast-growing social media sites.

Pure Digital Technologies started the "Flip experience" for potential customers by delivering fun in their messaging about recording, connecting, and sharing videos. Visiting their easy-to-navigate website was fun and inspiring. The site was about people, the Flip, and what the Flip could do for you. Whether people where looking at the new camera online or in a store, the promise of fun was at the forefront of the consumer message.

Between May 2007 and December 2008, Pure Digital Technologies generated $300 million in revenues from the sale of two million Flip Video cameras and garnered a seventeen percent share of the video camera market. The Flip Ultra video camera created a new market segment, the point-and-shoot video camera. It caught large, well-established companies like Sony, Canon, and Panasonic completely off-guard in the tenth consecutive year of flattening camcorder sales. Sony's existing market share,

> **THE FLIP'S** customer experience was ELEGANT as well as **FUN.** Customers could now **RECORD,** CONNECT, and **SHARE** their videos quickly and EASILY, almost anywhere they **WANTED.**

21 percent at the time, began to decline. The Flip video camera had a reasonable price and delivered on its promise with a rewarding customer experience before, during, and after the purchase. At the end of the summer of 2010, almost five million Flip video cameras had been sold.

The Flip's customer experience was elegant as well as fun. Flip owners could record, connect, and share their videos quickly and easily, almost anywhere they wanted. And customers were not the only ones who appreciated the experience. "The ease of use is incredibly seductive," said

Paul Ryder, Amazon's Vice President of Electronics.

Many people, including some video enthusiasts, industry experts, and media analysts, were baffled by the increasing sales momentum of the Flip. Why didn't the Flip have more features? Kaplan's response: "We're not going to add features and functions." The Flip was a better product to its five million-plus customers because of its simplicity and the experience it offered people. It did what users wanted, and did it well. In a 2009 article in *Wired*, Vice President of Marketing at Pure Digital Technologies, Simon Fleming-Wood, defines quality of the Flip in terms of ease of use. "The one thing everyone wants to do with their footage is show it to someone else," says Fleming-Wood.

This doesn't mean that the company wasn't open to adding capabilities to the Flip. Since the Flip's inception, the company has added high definition resolution and a better-quality LCD screen. Flip owners can personalize the exterior of the camera with colors and special designs.

One whole year passed after the introduction of the Flip before Sony had its competitive answer to the product. The *Wall Street Journal* said that the introduction of the Webbie, later to be renamed Bloggie, "symbolizes an important shift in Sony's culture." Sony was not alone, as the list of Flip imitators grew, with names like Kodak Playsport, JVC Picaso, Vivitar Pocket Video, and Samsung HMX.

SURPRISE ACQUISITION BY CISCO

In March 2009, Pure Digital Technologies was purchased by Cisco for $590 million in stock and $15 million in retention-based equity incentives. Cisco is a $40 billion publicly-traded company with over 73,400 employees in 165 countries.

Cisco's reputation, profitability, and culture centers

on producing and selling industrial equipment that routes and switches data inside the networks of large communications devices. The company has prospered by providing industrial equipment that typically has much higher profit margins, complexity, and longer sales and life cycles than consumer electronics. Data switches are Cisco's leading product line, with over 70 percent of the market. The company dominates the router equipment market with over 50 percent of that market. Cisco also participates in security, data storage networks, web conferencing, and voice communications markets. Compared to the large businesses it serves with complex industrial communications products, its consumer business, which includes video, set-top boxes, and home routers, has never done well.

Cisco's strategy, according to John Chambers, Chairman and CEO, in a presentation in June 2011, is "based on catching market transitions that affect our customers." The company does this by building, partnering, or buying what it needs to get there. Cisco claims that it applies for over 700 patents annually and has at least 8,000 issued in its name. The company also states in its public communications that it meets or exceeds it major rivals IBM, Microsoft, Intel, and Hewlett-Packard in research and development spending as percentage of annual revenues. Cisco wasted no time after its acquisition of Pure Digital Technologies to start converting the assignment of patents from Pure Digital Technologies, Jonathan Kaplan, Ariel Braunstein and others to Cisco.

It was not clear to many experts in the communications or consumer electronics industries what market transitions Cisco was trying to catch by acquiring Pure Digital Technologies. Many commentators remarked on the lack of a fit between the two businesses. While the sales of the Flip continued to increase post-merger, there was a lack of synergies between Cisco and Pure Digital Technologies.

In early 2011, the Flip continued to be one of the most recognized brand names in consumer electronics. Its momentum in the market and ability to convert customers to energized advocates was still increasing. The Flip's profitability as a consumer electronics product was very competitive. Market share estimates of the Flip ranged from 30 to 40 percent of total video camera sales. Flip was the best-selling video camera on Amazon.

With brisk sales and a strong outlook for demand, the people at Flip planned to release a new product with expanded networking capabilities while retaining the fantastic customer experience. It was an Internet camera and would be called the FlipLive. The new camera would use a wi-fi hot spot so users could broadcast live from anywhere they could get connected to the Internet. The FlipLive connection and location would create a clickable link that could be used by anyone on the Internet, possibly millions of people at once. Its introduction date was set for April 13, 2011.

THE FLIP IS GONE

On April 12, 2011, Cisco announced that its Flip Video business would be shut down. Shuttering the Flip business resulted in 550 layoffs and a pretax charge of about $300 million in the third and fourth quarter of the fiscal year. While Cisco did not offer a detailed explanation of why the Flip was suddenly gone, the announcement did make it clear that the closure decision was a strategic "part of the company's comprehensive plan to align its operations" and "that it will exit aspects of its consumer businesses and realign the remaining consumer business to support four of its five key company priorities: core routing, switching and services; collaboration; architectures; and video."

The announcement came when Cisco's quarterly net income decreased from $2.2 billion to $1.8 billion. Earnings per share for the quarter were down 12 percent to 33 cents, compared with 37 cents in the same quarter of fiscal year 2010. Many people close to the company felt that its drive to pursue growth, including growth through acquisition, was more of a distraction than a disciplined execution of strategy linked to actual opportunities.

On April 22, ten days after Cisco announced the Flip would no longer exist, registered owners of Flip cameras received an e-mail: "Thank you Flip fans for all your support and comments about Flip and our team here as we begin our transition plans to close the business. However, do know we will continue to provide technical support for Flip video cameras until 12/31/2013 and Flip cameras will be available through our online and in-store retail partners as well as our Flip store while supplies last." The one-year warranty would still be upheld. Support for both hardware and software would be continued for a nominal fee and e-support would be continued to 12/31/13. The e-mail message ended with "The teams have been reading your comments from emails and our social media community pages and are touched by the overwhelming number of thoughts and messages. [Signed] *The Flip Video team*."

There was no explanation to all the Flip customers as to why Cisco suddenly pulled the plug on the high-growth business with a great brand and future outlook. Customers were deeply shocked. Competitors were confounded, too. Their sales in the market that the Flip created were increasing. In a statement published in *PCMag.com* just three days after Cisco's announcement, Kodak said it was "surprised" by Cisco's decision to eliminate the Flip. Kodak's sales in the personal video camera category grew

170 percent the previous year. "Pocket video cameras will continue to be a strong growth area," the company continued in the statement.

On one of Sony's blogs was a comment about point-and-shoot video competition from cell phones: "We won't play dumb on the idea of cell phone video entering the market but the reality is right now that we believe it's apples to oranges…We've seen a large demand for small, easy and affordable devices with edgy features like 3D video and dual screens."

The easy answer to why Cisco killed the Flip is that cell phones were providing too much competition to a stand-alone small video camera. But David Pogue, the *New York Times* technology columnist and blogger didn't see it that way. "Everybody's first reaction is: 'Oh, it's because of smartphones. Everybody's shooting video with iPhones nowadays—nobody's buying Flip camcorders,'" said Pogue in a *New York Times* blog post. Just a month earlier he was briefed by a Flip product manager about the new FlipLive camera to be introduced and was told that the Flip held 35 percent of the market and was selling fast.

"The most plausible reason is that Cisco wants the technology in the Flip more than it wants the business," said Pogue. "Cisco is, after all, in the videoconferencing business, and the Flip's video quality—for its size and price—was amazing. Maybe, in fact, that was Cisco's plan all along. Buy the beloved Flip for its technology, then shut it down and fire 550 people."

As of June 2011, a look at patent activity shows the process continuing for the reassignments of patents from Pure Digital Technologies, Jonathan Kaplan, Ariel Braunstein and others to Cisco.

The Flip was a unique and wonderful product, but did not belong in the Cisco family. Cisco's core competency is in industrial communication and networking, not personal retail products.

In that same *New York Times* blog post, Pogue added that Kaplan spoke to Pogue's Columbia Business School class one week after Cisco's announcement to shut down the Flip. Kaplan addressed the idea that the smartphone killed his baby by saying, "I don't think the smartphone was really at all involved. Camera phones haven't stopped over 35 million cameras a year from being sold in the U.S." Kaplan noted that the Flip was very profitable at Cisco. "It took in $500 million the first year." Kaplan's view was that the culprit was Cisco's stock price crashing, which was unusual for the company. "Cisco's shareholders wanted the company to focus on its core business." Kaplan confirmed that the Flip's technology was in fact being used on other Cisco products.

So the Flip is gone. "Is that fair to us? To the consumer? To the world? Probably not. But if Cisco manages to turn itself around, and the share prices go up, everyone will say that it was a really good decision," Kaplan said. Kaplan confirmed to Pogue's class that LG, Amazon, Hewlett-Packard, Sony, and Kodak all tried to buy Pure Digital Technologies.

From Video to Grilled Cheese

What's next for Kaplan? He plans to open five restaurants in San Francisco in 2011, then 500 more nationwide by 2015. They'll be called "The Melt." The company will use location-based mobile technology combined with upscale food offerings to try to create an excellent customer experience. The food served will be combos of grilled cheese and soup, including such items as "aged gruyere on white wheat with creamy wild mushroom soup" or "smoked gouda on eight grain bread with spicy black bean soup." An order can be placed from a mobile phone or computer and the customer will be sent a QR code as the order ID, which the customer will scan at the restaurant. Customers can pay through their phone and quickly pick up their orders. From reinventing the video camera market, Kaplan is moving on to reinvent fast food.

The Flip is dead. Long live The Melt!

TRAFFIC TICKETS STARTED A COMPANY

Another company that has been able to take a big share of its market by focusing on the customer experience and honing down the number of features in its products is I DRIVE SAFELY in Carlsbad, California.

In 1998, two colleagues each received traffic tickets. They both needed to attend traffic school. They knew that meant taking a course in a classroom for eight hours on a Saturday. It wasn't a big leap for them to realize there was a business opportunity in online offerings for traffic school. In less than one year, I DRIVE SAFELY was in operation.

I DRIVE SAFELY (IDS) currently services more than 700,000 customers every year. The 200-employee company has experienced a 40 percent annual growth rate from 2007 through 2010. The company is certified in more than thirty states for online driver's education, and does business in all fifty states and Canada. It serves three markets: teenagers, specialty drivers, and experienced drivers.

Co-founder and Managing Partner Gari Garimella says, "I would love to tell you that our sustained growth is achieved by working on some unique features and unique selling propositions. But it is our understanding of the audiences for our services and tailoring experiences for those specific audiences that drives it."

IDS makes sure to understand as much as possible

about its customers so the company can purposely engage those people with a customer experience that suits them. Most of the people IDS serves do not compare their options for online traffic courses based on features. They look for assurance of passing, approvals and price.

The main Do-Fors of IDS are: Courses that are simple, affordable, and hassle-free.

IDS builds the customer experience based on what each market segment is looking for. IDS segments the market by the types of experience the customers would like, regardless of the price. Garimella says, "We believe it is all about people's expectations. Everyone in the online traffic school market wants a good experience, even if they are shopping on price. And the expectation of the experience can vary greatly across a product category. We had to segment the market, to break it into sensible and well-defined pieces based on what people were buying and their expectations of the experience that would work best for them."

IDS Do-Fors for the teenage market are: the course must be easy, fast, and online, plus have assurances that they will pass the course for their first license. IDS makes it easy for teens to access contracts, guides, and how-to information and get it to their parents.

The customer experience is further tailored for mature drivers, and those who need to mitigate traffic tickets. Do-Fors for the experienced driver market (ages 55+): the course is easy to take and simple to complete. In the market for people who have received traffic tickets, the Do-Fors are: speed and convenience, ease of ordering, an approved program that will dismiss the points associated with the ticket, and express delivery for people who complete it at the last minute.

There are other competitors to IDS trying to add more features and lower prices. Those companies are losing their profit margins and customers to I DRIVE SAFELY. Garimella says, "They do not understand the customer expectations and markets as well as we do. Features do not equate directly to value. Some features provide value but it is in the context of the entire experience. You are not going to sell a Honda to the guy that wants and can buy the Ferrari. But if a guy wants to buy a Honda, he still needs a tailored, pleasing experience."

IDS recognizes that it is in the business of saving lives. That, according to Garimella, is the ultimate Do-For for I DRIVE SAFELY. "Understand the people who buy your products," says Garimella. "Know and anticipate their needs, wants, and how they make buying decisions. Then figure out what you can do to deliver it."

Feature creep

Whether a product or service starts out with an extraordinary customer experience or is trying to get there, feature creep can be a deadly enemy of a great experience. Feature creep is one of the main drivers in a product, especially for a software product, where the companies compete on giving more features and upgrades.

Phil Ohme of Intuit is aware of the danger of feature creep at his company. Says Ohme, "When someone is shopping for a new product, they look at the list of features and what they do. They usually want all the features they do not have. The companies respond by adding features. Then the companies react to each other's new features by creating more features."

Is FEATURE CREEP the **ENEMY** of a GOOD customer EXPERIENCE?

Ohme explains that many companies believe they can make more money if they can get people to upgrade every year. But since people don't upgrade every year, companies put more features in to encourage the upgrades. At a certain point, too many features make the overall product worse.

Is feature creep the enemy of a good customer experience? Ohme believes that "If there are so many features that solve everybody's needs, the product is not going to do one given task well." Ohme recalls Intuit's challenge to keep Quicken competitive, but feature creep and the law of diminishing returns beat them. "Quicken became bloated with features. Then one of our competitors, Mint, a provider of online personal finance services, got people set up with their personal finance products faster than we did. And that is what people wanted." Mint developed an easier and more intelligent way for people to manage their money. Customers responded and so did Intuit, buying privately-held Mint for an estimated $170 million in September 2009.

A SQUARE DEAL

A small company, Square, has used a better customer experience to differentiate itself from its competition and gain market share. Started by Twitter co-founder Jack Dorsey, Square offers a small, square-shaped credit card reader that plugs into the earphone jack of an iPhone, iPad, or Android smartphone. Rather than loading the reader with more features,  Square provided the simple Do-Fors that customers wanted: "Sign up for Square, get your free card reader in the mail, and start swiping. Accept all credit cards.

No hidden fees, no commitments—ever." Square makes money by charging merchants 2.75 percent of sales plus 15 cents for each card swipe. The company says it is adding 60,000 merchants a month.

Square's customer experience is very simple and easy. There is a one-page web form to complete to start accepting credit cards. The card reader itself is provided free of charge for anyone who signs up for the service.

Square's easy customer experience opened up the market for mobile credit card readers to a variety of businesses. According to a February 2011 article in *Bloomberg Businessweek*, the credit card readers are used by businesses as disparate as farm market vendors, a house call-making veterinarian, and heating system technicians who receive payments on site when the work is complete. The market for smartphone-based credit card transactions is expected to reach $55 billion by 2015, according to estimates by independent researcher Aite Group.

LEAVING COMPLEXITY BEHIND

The examples of Pure Digital Technologies' Flip, the online courses of I DRIVE SAFELY, and the easy credit card readers from Square show the great value that understanding and anticipating what people want a product or service to do for them can provide to a company. The Do-Fors that customers want can guide a company toward careful selection of features.

Although the Flip story doesn't have a happy ending, at least for the loyal Flip customers, it was a great success while it lasted. Sometimes forces outside a company's control will affect whether the company can continue to prosper, or even exist. Cisco clearly has made decisions about the Flip that don't reflect the exceptional customer experience that

Flip customers received during the product's heyday.

Pure Digital Technologies, I DRIVE SAFELY, and Square, three small smart companies, had access to ideas, technology, processes, people, and messages. They chose to leave complexity behind when selecting how they would determine, develop, and deliver greater customer experiences.

Chapter 5
The Emotional Connection

"Whatever one may think of the Mini Cooper's dynamic attributes, which range from very good to marginal, it is fair to say that almost no new vehicle in recent memory has provoked more smiles."

—NEW YORK TIMES, JUNE 2, 2002

SOME OF THE BEST CUSTOMER EXPERIENCES DELIBERATELY evoke strong emotions: attraction, trust, fun. Experiences with a strong emotional connection can create long-lasting customer relationships and fanatical advocates. The customer's connection with the experience is not solely based on logic. It can be a customer's personal reflection of the company and the brand.

BMW's Mini Cooper car is just such a product whose customer experience is built upon the customer's emotional connection with the product and the company.

In 1959, designer Alec Issigonis created the first Mini—a small family car with room for four adults that could also be driven like a sports car. The Mini became an icon for the swinging '60s in Britain.

Two million Minis were sold in the next decade, with truck and station wagon versions added to the race car-like sedan model. In the U.S., the Mini was discontinued with more stringent emissions regulations, but around the world, another two million Minis were sold by 1977.

In 1999, the Mini was voted "European Car of the Century" by international automotive writers, and second only to the Ford Model T for the global title. But in 2000, sales of the Mini had declined to the point where the car's production was discontinued. BMW brought back the brand in 2002, changing its image from entry level to premium, and reintroducing it to the U.S. market. The Mini was named the 2003 North American Car of the Year and has gained a following in the U.S. since then. In March 2011, BMW sold 7,689 Minis, sixteen percent more than the sales for the same period in 2007. To meet the increasing demand for Mini models, the company's assembly plant is expected to increase its annual production to 240,000 vehicles.

Why is the Mini so popular and influential? There are plenty of small family cars in the market. Why does the Mini make us *smile*?

The Mini Cooper engineers *intentionally* redesigned and rethought everything about the car and the experience to keep its customers happy and engaged with its quirkiness and attractiveness. The Mini Cooper provides basic transportation, getting from point A to point B, but the experience is exciting and fun. The customer experience was created *on* purpose and *with* purpose.

Owners of the Mini Cooper have long been known to be one of the most fanatical and loyal of all car owners. Mini Cooper owners are to car ownership what Apple owners are to personal electronics. They actively participate in local motoring clubs and are a passionate and faithful community. The "Coop" has the same instruments any other car has, but they are quirky, friendly forms with a funky, modern feel and sometimes unorthodox (and even non-ergonomic) arrangement, like the larger central "spee-do" pod. The layout of the dashboard may not be the most efficient, but it helps to provide a fully engaging *experience*. The Mini Cooper makes driving fun!

The Mini Cooper experience doesn't begin or end with the car alone. Mini has crafted the experience of how customers engage and interact with sales people, customer service reps, and the website. From advertising, social media, going online, signing on, reading the humorous content, designing your own Mini, ordering the car, following the production and delivery of the car online, and even the unveiling of your car at the dealership—it is totality of the thoughtful experience purposely executed.

Mini customers are having great experiences, not only driving the car, but also at the dealerships. It is not uncommon to see online customer reviews for Mini that say: "I've bought well over twenty cars in my life, and I would say the local Mini dealer was easily one of the best I've ever dealt with." Mini invests heavily in the customer experience training of its staff, and the company is constantly measuring the dealership experience to ensure that it is great. A Mini Cooper dealership is clean, professional, and a little funky, like the car. The people who work there are laid-back, courteous, and professional.

Mini doesn't leave anything to chance. The company has a sophisticated internal system that is used to constantly measure this dealership experience. Mini Cooper surveys its customers and creates a Customer Service Index (CSI) score for their sales and service staff. If a customer has an issue, a staff member must respond within 24 hours. All the dealership employees know their scores and can monitor them in real time on their intranet, logging into *minimotoringexperience.com* to track their CSI scores. Mini sales reps' bonuses are determined by these scores.

When you ask owners about their Minis, they talk about the experience of *buying* it as much as they talk about driving the car, its performance, or gas mileage. Think about that—Mini has made the process of paying your hard-earned money a fun experience!

Because the majority of Minis are designed by the customer to include custom options, most Mini Cooper dealerships keep relatively few cars in stock. This designed-by-the-customer aspect provides a strong emotional attachment to the car. But the wait for the completed car can be tough on the prospective Mini owner. To alleviate the pain of waiting, Mini has a website that allows customers to follow the progress of their cars from the time of ordering to the day of delivery. At the website's "owner's lounge," customers track the status of their cars through six steps: on order, scheduled for production, awaiting transport, en route, at distribution center, and at the Mini dealer.

Customers can call Mini anytime for more detailed information about their cars and can speak with a representative who can tell them exactly what is happening with their cars at that moment. And with "Ship Tracker," customers can even track their own cars' trip across the ocean. Customers can even chat on a forum with other customers who are having their cars manufactured at the same time—sharing in each other's experience as they join the Mini Cooper league of zealots.

Understanding emotions

An emotional connection is formed with every aspect of the relationship with the consumer: from the promises in the first ad the person sees, to the experience of the company's website, to how a company representative responds on the phone, to the experience of making a purchase, to how the customer perceives the touch and use of the products and services. It includes all the experiences a person has interacting with a business.

The data tells us that emotions affect our decision-making. Donald Norman, author of *Emotional Design: Why We Love (or Hate) Everyday Things*, is one of the leading authorities on emotion and design. *Business Week* labeled him a "cantankerous visionary" and has listed him as one of the world's most influential designers. In his book, Norman suggests that emotions influence product design. "When people are anxious they tend to narrow their thought processes, concentrating upon aspects directly relevant to a problem. When people are relaxed and happy, their thought process expands, becoming creative, more imaginative." Norman concludes, "Happy people are more effective in finding alternative solutions and are tolerant of minor difficulties."

The Mini Cooper is an interesting example of how emotion influences customer experience. Plenty of Mini owners complain about the location of the radio or fact that the speedometer is much larger than it needs to be, but because of the *fun* of the total experience of the Mini, they tolerate the car's quirks. The positive emotional experience affects their decision-making. They are happy driving their Mini Cooper and even convince themselves that they like the quirks.

The data tells us that people will actually rationalize their decision based on how they feel. According to Norman, the research shows that emotions provide critical assistance to our decision making by helping us make rapid selections between good and bad, reducing the number of things to be considered. Norman explains that, "Cognition interprets and understands the world around you, while emotions make value judgments, deciding, among other things, what's good or bad, safe or dangerous."

Ivan Crespo is an engineer with a passion for making customers happy. Ivan is a software R&D Engineering Manager at Eastman Kodak and has worked at other major technology companies. Crespo recounts a lesson he learned at a company earlier in his career. The company he then worked for had a software application that allowed people to manage their photos. This application was consistently rated higher with potential customers than competitors' software. It was found to be quicker and easier on several standard measures. But when asked to choose between this application and competitors' products, people actually preferred the competition. Crespo realized that "the emotional component—how the application presented itself, what kind of relationship people had with the other application—made a huge difference with how people reacted to it. That was the biggest 'Aha!' that we had." Like the Mini Cooper, that visceral, emotional connection outweighed how easy it was to use—that form could trump function when form is brilliant. The

> **PEOPLE** make **PURCHASE DECISIONS** about how they **FEEL** about THINGS. And if the feeling is strong enough, they **WILL** justify their decisions to **SUPPORT** their EMOTIONAL CONNECTION.

application's ease of use was not enough for customers to select the product. "We had to think not only about the functional side of the app, but also the emotional design."

The emotional connection that customers make with a company's products and services is just as important, or more important, than making an efficient product or delivering an effective service. The emotional connection shapes peoples' perceptions of the company, its products, services, and brand. People make purchase decisions about how they *feel* about things. And if the feeling is strong enough, they will justify their decisions to support their emotional connection.

THE CUSTOMER'S EMOTIONAL JOURNEY

Kaaren Hanson, Vice President of Design Innovation at Intuit, says that at Intuit they give great consideration to emotion. "We have emotion journey maps where we deliberately map out what we want the emotion to be," says Hanson. "We look a lot at where there are negative or neutral parts that we can make positive. We think about the emotional journey over time for the customer."

When people are anxious and doing a task they dread, like paying taxes, understanding their emotional journey can lead to innovative solutions. Intuit's SnapTax is a mobile application that runs on an iPhone or Android. When filling out the 1040EZ, SnapTax allows you to snap a photo of your W-2 with your mobile device. It imports your information, then the customer answers a few quick questions, reviews, files, and it's done. Says Hanson, "People can get their taxes filed in seconds. All they have to do is snap a picture. The rush from that is amazing. One of the reasons they feel such a rush is that it is so innovative and surprising. Here they are doing their taxes and dreading that, and then they have a great experience."

Intuit examined all the emotional connections along the customers' journey and found solutions that made it easy and removed the dread from the experience. Intuit's "emotion journey maps" identify all the customers' emotional touch points with the experience and measure those touch points based on emotional responses. Intuit runs studies in its labs to record customers interacting with Intuit products, measuring facial cues for happiness and frustration.

CREATING ENDURING RELATIONSHIPS WITH CUSTOMERS

In Claudel Arguin's 2010 thesis, *Emotional Durability Is the New Sustainability: Why Are Objects Cherished Even after Their Functionality Has Been Surpassed*, he describes the stages of relationships with products and services. These stages along the customer's journey are opportunities to purposely create positive emotional connections.

The *first encounter* is a strong factor in shaping a customer's expectation of the product or service relationship. There are many ways to discover a product or service in the first stage of the relationship. Someone may hear about it from a friend, or see an advertisement in a magazine, on television, or on the Internet. The first encounter can be an "impulse" reaction—an instant attraction or repulsion. The company, of course, wants it to be the beginning of a long, happy relationship full of fun, delight, and trust. This is the point along the journey to transform prospects to customers. Companies who purposely craft the customer experience understand this first encounter and work at building a positive emotional connection right away. Today's experience makers are on top of the conversations that customers are having about their brand. They actively monitor and participate in these discussions and capitalize on their advocates' praises. They use the advocates' "voices" in their advertisements and ensure that the first message a prospective customer hears is the one the company has crafted.

The second stage is *commitment*—choosing to purchase the product or service. In this stage, people have two different approaches: a researched purchase or an impulse purchase. Consumers make researched purchases for big-ticket items that are expensive. Though these are educated decisions, they are also deeply personal. The home and car are often seen as extensions of our personality, and we form strong, long-lasting connections. Mini Cooper understands this concept. The company thoughtfully builds the entire purchasing interaction between the customer and the sales people, customer service reps, and the web. Customers do their research about the car—looking at print and Internet advertising, reading the content on the Mini Cooper website, discussing the car in social media, designing their own Mini, ordering the car, following the production and delivery of the car online, and the unveiling of the car at the dealership—which all help customers develop very positive emotional connections with the Mini Cooper.

Impulse purchases, on the other hand, are based on quick decisions. Emotion helps customers make the decision quickly. Apple's iTunes, Amazon's books, or Netflix movies all exemplify that impulse reaction—"I've got to have that"—and ensure a strong emotional connection in the commitment stage of the customer relationship.

Regardless of whether it is a well-researched decision or an impulse purchase, a strong relationship will only endure if the emotional connection lingers. After the purchase, the next stage is the *honeymoon period*, where the product or service is put to the test. This is when the customer discovers how much he or she enjoys the product or service. Following this period, the relationship moves to the final stage, which is either to **endure** or **break down**. If a company consistently delivers a better experience than its competition, then customers will develop a high level of trust with the company and the brand. If the company consistently delivers a *great* experience, then the company has won a long-lasting customer and advocate who will likely tell other potential customers. If the promise was not met, then the company has lost that customer, who is equally likely to tell other people not to buy the product.

EMOTIONAL CONNECTION SECURES THE BRAND AND TRUST

Your brand can either draw your customer towards your products and services or away from it. Sergio Zyman, former Chief Marketing Officer of Coca-Cola, wrote about "emotional branding" in the foreword to Marc Gobe's book, *Emotional Branding: The New Paradigm for Connecting Brands to People*. Zyman said, "Emotional branding is about building relationships; it is about giving a brand and a product long-term value. Emotional branding is based on that unique trust that is established with an audience. It elevates purchases based on need to the realm of desire."

Smart companies are building relationships with their brand to create long-term value. They are developing enduring emotional connections with their customers to secure their brand and trust. Gary Tucker, Senior Vice President at J.D. Power and Associates, says that in terms of brand and developing trust, "customer experience, by definition, is a sustainable advantage." Tucker considers how the automotive industry has evolved. He says, "Ten years ago, if you went onto the J.D. Power site, it was obvious which car to buy and which car not to buy. Today, it is not clear that there is a car that I should or should not buy. More emotional considerations come into play for that decision and experience, both real and perceived, that are going to have tremendous influence."

Delivering the right customer experience creates a sustainable brand that is hard for competitors to duplicate. And consumers will pay more for it. Tucker explains this idea: "If you are a retail bank, how much is product innovation going to drive deposit growth? You can come up with the next new cool product, but in sixty to ninety days, the guy on the next corner will also have that product. Anyone can copy it. But if you build a model around service, and hire and train the right people to deliver the right experience, that is a more sustainable competitive advantage, and we know from the data that people will pay for it."

> Customer experience, by **DEFINITION**, is a SUSTAINABLE ADVANTAGE.

Value is created through personal attachment. A brand can either draw a customer towards a product or away from it. The emotional connection created with a customer builds relationships and gives your product long-term value.

Provoke smiles.

Chapter 6
Innovating Customer Experiences

"We're connecting people with the movies they love."

—Steve Swasey, Netflix

To be a customer experience leader, you don't have to invent a new technology. But if you can fit existing and emerging technologies to customer needs, you can innovate the customer experience to the point that you can take over the market.

That's the story of two companies profiled here, Netflix and LPL. Both companies innovated the customer experience itself, and in doing so, created whole new business categories.

Netflix has dominated the business of providing videos to consumers for a decade, slaying a giant in the industry—Blockbuster—in the process. In mid-2011, the narrative of Netflix has changed, and Netflix is experiencing severe challenges to its business. In this chapter, we'll describe how Netflix created an outstanding customer experience that revolutionized the video rental industry.

The other company, LPL, is less well known to the

public at large but has made a huge impact on the brokerage industry by employing some of the same techniques used by Netflix in its early days. LPL has innovated the customer experience for the brokerage industry, and in doing so, has created a new category of brokerage firm that allows independent financial advisors to compete directly with the major firms.

Two companies with similar stories: innovating the customer experience to change their industries forever.

Enter Netflix

April 14, 1998. Not one of the twelve people standing in the checkout line to rent movies in the Blockbuster store has any idea that a new customer experience will soon change they way they rent movies.

As those people move up the line at Blockbuster past the popcorn, Dots, and Sno-Cap candies, a start-up company called Netflix has just announced the opening of the world's first Internet store to offer movie rentals. The announcement promises that virtually every movie will be available on DVD, a new movie format. Movie enthusiasts can now enjoy the convenience of movie rental online.

How could a freshly-funded company less than two years old create a serious challenge to a well-entrenched giant like Blockbuster? The answer is in the customer experience.

The first Blockbuster video rental store opened on Oct 19, 1985, in Dallas, Texas. At that time, most video rental businesses were small, independently-owned stores with a limited selection of movies. By contrast, the earliest Blockbusters were three times larger than the biggest competitor, offering a selection of 3,000 to 8,000 titles. But Blockbusters were run similarly to the small independents: they were basically movie libraries. This library experience, including check-ins, check-outs, and the dreaded penalty fees, was not much different than a book library. The penalty fees increased over time and Blockbuster grew to depend on late fees as a profit center.

The company's founder, David Cook, sold his stores to a group of investors. One of those investors was Wayne Huizenga, the founder of Waste Management, Inc., the world's largest garbage disposal company. Huizenga soon became the sole owner of Blockbuster. Huizenga began to acquire independently-owned video stores and grew Blockbuster quickly. In 1988, Blockbuster was the leading video chain in the U.S., with 400 stores. By the early 1990s, the Blockbuster chain had 1,000 retail stores and had expanded overseas. In September 1993, Blockbuster became part of media giant Viacom Inc., alongside MTV and Nickelodeon. Huizenga left the company in September 1994.

Blockbuster went through one CEO each year until the spring of 1997, when John Antioco took the helm. The company was in rough condition after several grandiose missteps, including attempts to grow by adding music, computer software, video games, and international expansion. By the second quarter of 1997, Blockbuster's cash flow was reduced by 70 percent. Viacom was disappointed with Blockbuster's growth rate. The company had planned to use the cash from Blockbuster to help other parts of Viacom's business. Since this was no longer an option, Viacom sold Blockbuster for $115 million in August 1998—the same year that the DVD was introduced.

In 1998, Blockbuster had over 6,000 retail stores in 26 countries, and 60 million active subscribers and 80,000 employees. Blockbuster's worldwide revenue reached $3.89 billion with losses of $336.6 million. Blockbuster took note of its new competition, Netflix (without naming names), in its 1999 annual report: "We are also moving forward to realize the opportunities presented by e-commerce and new direct-to-home technologies." But it was six years after Netflix entered the market before Blockbuster effectively started its online DVD rental program in the U.S.

THE BLOCKBUSTER CUSTOMER EXPERIENCE

Blockbuster was clearly dedicated to running its retail stores, which preserved the library experience for customers, whether customers liked it or not. Interestingly, at first, Blockbuster had been an innovator. Unlike the independent video rental shops, Blockbuster's video rental store experience was consistent from store to store. It provided a family-friendly environment. The videos were displayed throughout the store on categorized shelves, rather than behind the counter. Inventory and rented videos were tracked by an automated system.

But one feature that really hurt the customer experience was the penalty fees levied on Blockbuster customers. Fees for returning videos late or for not rewinding the VHS tape were a source of profits to Blockbuster. To customers, these fees were a source of worry, anger, and frustration. People felt pressured to view the movies in three days or pay a fine. In addition, the Blockbuster customer experience began with a time-consuming errand, leaving home to rent a movie at a Blockbuster store.

THE NETFLIX CUSTOMER EXPERIENCE

It was Reed Hastings's unpleasant customer experience as a video renter that inspired him to start Netflix. Interviewed on *60 Minutes* in 2006, Hastings confessed his genesis of the Netflix idea: "I'd rented a VHS (*Apollo 13*) and I had misplaced it and it was six weeks late. So it was a $40 late fee. I didn't want to tell my wife. And I thought, 'Oh, great! Now I'm thinking about lying to my wife about a late fee and the sanctity of my marriage for this thing!' I mean it was just crazy. On the way to the gym I realized, 'Whoa! Video stores could operate like a gym, with a flat membership fee. I wonder why no one's done that before?'"

Hastings investigated the idea of a subscription service, where VHS movie cassettes would be shipped to customers. But the round-trip shipping cost of $12 was too expensive for the idea to work.

Then he learned about a new technology called the DVD, a CD with a movie on it that was not as delicate and bulky as a VHS tape. "I ran down to Tower (Records) and bought a bunch and mailed them to myself and then I waited," Hastings recalls. He wanted to see if they would get destroyed in the mail. "And I opened them up. And they were fine. And I thought, 'This is gonna work! This is gonna work!'"

Hastings paired the DVD with postal delivery to create the Netflix offer. Netflix's special agreement with the U.S. Post Office gave quick delivery of the movies to customers' mailboxes. An easy-to-use website with a large database of movies added to the Netflix experience.

Netflix's goal was not just to overcome what was unsatisfying about the video rental experience, but to remake that experience. Steve Swasey, Netflix's Vice-President of Corporate Communications, explains: "Netflix changed the way Americans view movies. Before Netflix you had to go to a video store to rent movies, you had to pay late fees which were punitive, you had pretty crummy service, and you had pretty limited selection. Netflix changed the whole rental business by making every title available and making it very cost effective with no return due dates and late fees whatsoever. You never have to leave your home. Login wherever you have your computer and the movies come to you. The convenience, selection, and value completely upended the entire movie rental industry and Netflix was the catalyst for that."

By December 1999, Netflix eliminated all due dates and late fees, charging members a set monthly fee for a set number of DVD rentals per month. Within the first year, the Do-Fors at the center of the customer experience at the Netflix online store were:

- The convenience of home shopping with the efficiencies of an online store
- Informative content, easy-to-use site navigation and search capabilities, low-cost delivery methods and competitive pricing
- Personalized merchandising and recommendations based on previous shopping sessions
- No due dates and the elimination of late fees

Netflix included "FlixFinder," so shoppers could search by title, actor, or director and instantly see a corresponding list of movies. "FilmFacts," gave a movie synopsis, ratings, and descriptions of the movie content, to make movie selection easier. Netflix also included "Browse the Aisles," to let customers scan lists of movies grouped around a common element, such as theme or genre. Personalizing movie recommendations was done with very sophisticated software for each subscriber called "Personalized Merchandising."

In the company's 2002 Annual Report, Hastings pointed to Netflix's superior competitive position compared to other online DVD subscription services, such as Walmart. com, Blockbuster, subscription entertainment services including HBO and Showtime, pay-per-view and video on demand providers, and cable and satellite providers. "We are able to provide greater subscriber satisfaction due to the broader and deeper selection of titles, including our ability to personalize our selection to each subscriber based on the subscriber's selection history; personal ratings and the tastes and preferences of similar users through our recommendation service, and extensive database of user preferences; as well as the ease and speed by which subscribers are able to select, receive and return titles."

By early 2009, ten years after the subscription service was launched, Netflix surpassed ten million subscribers. Over that time period, annual subscription growth was just under 30 percent. For eight of those ten years Netflix was rated the number one customer experience on the Internet by independent research firm ForeSee Results.

The Netflix customer experience changed the industry and people's expectations of renting movies. People were happy to permanently leave their frustrating experience of Blockbuster's retail and penalty-centric operation. And they did. In September 2010, Blockbuster filed for bankruptcy to reorganize under a Chapter 11 petition. The company listed assets of $1.02 billion against debt of $1.46 billion. It was all over for Blockbuster by early April 2011. Dish Network Corp. won a bankruptcy auction for Blockbuster Inc., offering approximately $320.6 million for the movie-rental chain. Some of its creditors split just $178.8 million of Dish's bid.

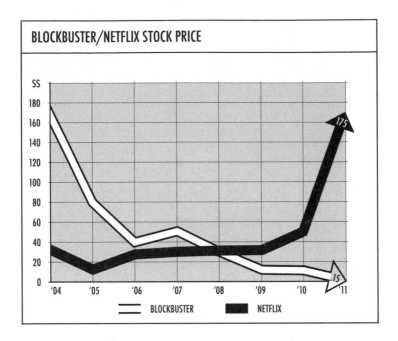

BLOCKBUSTER/NETFLIX STOCK PRICE

REACHING THE CROSSROAD

Companies sometimes reach a crossroad where they have to make a choice between the technologies and processes they currently use to deliver products or services and technologies and processes preferred by customers. If the company anticipates the crossroad, it can make the decision to change course successfully. But if a company reaches the crossroad unaware of changes in the market environment, or more committed to certain technologies than the experience of their customers, or preoccupied with other issues, it will likely falter.

Today, Netflix stands at a crossroad in technology—Internet streaming and instant delivery of movies via a variety of home devices. Netflix first made content available through a device other than a television in 2008. By 2010, the list of additional ways people could access movies included Xbox, PS3, Blu-ray players, Nintendo Wii, and iPads. According to Swasey, "Pretty soon you won't have to get off the couch because the Netflix button will be planted on the remote for DVD and Blu-ray. All you will have to do is push the red Netflix button to watch a movie."

Not one of Netflix's 25 million subscribers in the U.S. had any idea that their long and extraordinary customer experience would soon be shattered by a very unlikely source.

On July 12, 2011, Netflix changed that experience with one announcement. "Netflix to Offer New Unlimited DVD Plans and Will Separate Streaming and DVD Plans in the U.S. New Unlimited DVD-Only Plan at $7.99 is the Lowest-Ever Price Offered; Unlimited Streaming Remains $7.99." Suddenly, Netflix customers were forced to pay sixty percent more for the service they had been receiving, or make a choice between delivery methods for their video entertainment. And price was only part of the sudden deconstruction of Netflix's customer experience. The brand itself was broken, and additional work was created for customers.

Netflix has always defined its business by its Do-Fors: connecting people with the movies and entertainment they love. Now the experience became not what Netflix was doing FOR the customers, but what it was doing TO them.

Customer response was swift and strong. More than one million subscribers in the U.S. cancelled their Netflix accounts. The stock price plummeted 57 percent in two months, from $298.73 on July 13, 2011 to $129.36 by September 23.

The anger, betrayal, and confusion customers felt intensified when customers read a letter sent to them by Netflix CEO Reed Hastings September 19. "I messed up. I owe you an explanation." The letter went on to disorient people about the company's future and the brand. "In a few weeks, we will rename our DVD by mail service to 'Qwikster.' We chose the name 'Qwikster' because it refers to quick delivery. We will keep the name 'Netflix' for streaming." The letter acknowledged that Netflix's customers were angry and felt betrayed. "Both the Qwikster and Netflix teams will work hard to regain your trust. We know it will not be overnight. Actions speak louder than words. But words help people to understand actions."

Hastings's mea culpa letter didn't change customer sentiment. Most of the 27,000 responses on the Netflix blog in the first week showed that Hastings's letter was received as a late and hollow apology about the price increases. Splitting off the DVD business to new service called Qwikster was even more upsetting to Netflix's loyal customer base. The new name jettisoned DVD customers from all the good things that the Netflix brand stood for. One very annoyed customer framed the situation this way: "Splitting Netflix in two so that you have Netflix and Qwikster is the worst business decision since New Coke...Right now you have complete convenience on your site. I can look at any movie and see if it's available on DVD or Instant or both. I can right there at that moment make the decision on how to view it, but now instead of it being simple and easy, I have to go to two different sites. No customer will be happy that they now have to do twice as much for the same result."

The separation of the two delivery methods meant price increases for customers who wanted both services, as well as two different websites to navigate when ordering content, and two different bills for customers to pay. At the time of the announcement, more than twelve million Netflix customers received content by both streaming and DVDs.

On October 10, 2011, Netflix made another

announcement to its subscribers: "It is clear that for many of our members two websites would make things more difficult, so we are going to keep Netflix as one place to go for streaming and DVDs. This means no change: one website, one account, one password…in other words, no Qwikster."

Netflix is trying to get its customer experience right again. The company listened to its customers and quickly reversed the plan to break the service into two separate businesses, websites, and experiences for the customer.

Other companies known for creating extraordinary customer experiences have lost their way and found it again. Starbucks, Apple, and Intuit have all been there and come back. Those companies had the ability to recover by defining their situation realistically, then regaining their relevance, value, and customer experience advantage in a timely way. Netflix's customers decided that Netflix made tremendous miscalculations in decisions that affect the customer experience. Netflix has backed off, regrouped, and changed its course. As we have seen with other companies, the market will render the final decision.

THE CUSTOMER EXPERIENCE LIFECYCLE

The customer experience relevance and value can be inspired, shaped, and terminated by forces inside or outside the company. The company creating the customer experience is in direct control as a force on the customer experience lifecycle. But other forces outside the company have indirect control—time, technology, and competition.

The company competes with itself to offer a more significant and valuable customer experience, a "next generation" experience that supplants its own. When the company goes the other way, prematurely shocking or terminating the customer experience without a transition, it can destroy the value of its customer experience. Doing so can give the advantage to competitors that are ready to take over the experience lifecycle.

For Netflix, digital delivery created the crossroad where Netflix could be separated from its customers. Netflix participates in a market where changes are almost constant. Cooperation with the competition can blur the lines between partner and competitor. One example is Netflix's relationship with Amazon. The company depends on Amazon Web Services (AWS) to operate parts of its service. As described in Netflix's 2010 Annual Report, "Any disruption of or interference with our use of AWS would impact our operations and our business would be adversely impacted." But Amazon's retail business is a strong competitor to Netflix. The effectiveness of "Chinese walls" in business may become another outside force on Netflix's ability to compete in the future.

THE FUTURE OF NETFLIX

Why would a company that worked so hard to achieve extraordinary customer experiences for thirteen consecutive years deconstruct that experience? Does Netflix have a better experience on the other side? If so, why wasn't there a smoother transition from one experience to the other?

As of this writing, there is plenty of speculation about why Netflix would shock its exemplary customer experience. Reasons suggested include harvesting profit as the DVD business winds down, or separating the profit and loss statements for each line of business to position for mergers and acquisitions.

From the beginning of Netflix's success, there have been several companies that claim they can displace

Netflix—Amazon, Apple, Walmart, and even Dish, the company that bought Blockbuster's assets in April 2011.

Today, Apple is the biggest player in individual film transactions, accounting for sixty percent of them, according to IHS Screen Digest. Apple is generating more money for the movie studios than many cable companies, and is expected to become the largest provider of video on demand by 2014. Meanwhile, Amazon has built its own video subscription service to go head-to-head with Netflix. The launch of Amazon's own movie service started with offering 5,000 films and television programs to stream online. This video streaming service is available through Amazon Prime, the company's premium shipping service that gives customers unlimited shipping for $79 a year. "They're going to be able to watch movies without leaving Amazon or going somewhere else," according to Cameron Janes, Amazon's director of Instant Video, as quoted in the *Financial Times* in February 2011. Millions of customers have already signed up for the service. Amazon plans to expand the streaming service as they innovate the customer experience that goes with it. And Walmart may re-enter the movie distribution market. The company acquired Vudu video, giving its digital movie offerings and access to many preferred consumer electronic devices.

As of September 2011, Morningstar estimated that Netflix's U.S. subscriber base will grow to 41.6 million by 2015, with 33 percent of U.S. television households. Morningstar says Netflix is still very solid financially.

With the competitive door opened by Netflix, and with competitors vying for Netflix's angry, betrayed, and confused customers, the market is ripe for competitors. But the issue is not just about price. Customers are not in the mood for empty promises.

Can competitors deliver an extraordinary customer

experience to change the video rental landscape? Will that experience include commercial-free viewing of the content people love on their preferred devices?

Netflix is a company founded on innovation, which is the introduction, creation, or offering of something new and untraditional. Customer experience innovation can create or transform an industry and change peoples' lives for the better. Reed Hastings began Netflix with the realization that a video store could operate like a gym with flat fees. He used that concept to innovate the entire customer experience of renting videos. Will Netflix recover by innovating its next generation customer experience? Or will someone else pick up the lifecycle from Netflix and innovate the customer experience in pleasing ways we can't yet imagine? We'll leave this story now, but it isn't over yet...

HEAD TO HEAD WITH FINANCIAL GIANTS

If you were a stockbroker with an entrepreneurial heart and an independent soul, there were not many companies in the 1980s that would support your passions. That changed in 1989 when Todd Robinson, a former Smith Barney broker, created LPL Financial. He decided to build a company on his deep-seated belief that independent financial advisors should be able to offer objective advice, free of conflict, to their clients.

LPL Financial provides independent financial advisors with the technology, research, service, and support for their own businesses. LPL Financial does not have investment products of its own and is not affiliated with any bank. LPL Financial is very different from other financial companies like Merrill Lynch, Edward Jones, Morgan Stanley, and Charles Schwab. In those companies, financial advisors are employees. At LPL Financial, they are customers.

Robinson founded the company by combining two small financial companies, Linsco and Private Ledger, into Linsco Private Ledger (LPL). Known today as LPL Financial, the structure of the firm is totally opposite that of the big brokerage houses—the advisor sets up his/her independent investment advising business, and LPL Financial essentially functions as the advisor's "back office." The independent investment advisor chooses from a wide range of LPL Financial resources available to support the investment practice, including technology, research, training, practice management, and succession planning, to name a few.

As of year-end 2010, LPL Financial reached annual revenues of $3.1 billion and total advisory and brokerage assets of over $300 billion. The company has over 2,700 employees and has amassed over 12,700 financial advisors, as of September 2011.

LPL Financial competes in an enormous market. Over $10.4 trillion in retail assets are professionally managed, according to research firm Cerulli Associates. LPL Financial, whose advisors work with more than four million customers that on average have assets from $100,000 to $1 million to invest, now ranks as the largest independent broker/dealer in the U.S., based on revenue as reported in *Financial Planning* magazine. The number of advisors is shrinking at many big firms, while LPL Financial has almost tripled its number of advisors during the last ten years. LPL Financial's advisors have constantly ranked among the best in the last three years of J.D. Power's U.S. Full Service Investor Satisfaction Study.

Esther Stearns, President and Chief Operating Officer of LPL Financial, says that from the start, "we thought about empowering entrepreneurs and independent financial advisors. We wanted to provide them business opportunities and capabilities that were better than the employees of the wirehouses."

The wirehouses, such as Morgan Stanley, Merrill Lynch, and UBS, were large, multi-office brokerage firms that used advanced communications to transmit customer orders for execution. They had their own computer systems that were integrated with their communications systems. This was the distinct advantage of the wirehouses over the smaller brokerage firms, allowing them to be very efficient at placing, tracking, and reporting customer's transactions. The wirehouses were entrenched and had networks and computer servers that could handle huge amounts of information. They could deliver data and capabilities directly into their large centralized offices. They had plenty of money to spend on technology infrastructure and offers that independents couldn't compete with.

In its early years, LPL Financial took advantage of the burgeoning Internet technology to build systems that provided independent advisors with the same kinds of data and services previously only available at wirehouse firms. Stearns emphasizes that in 1996, "we believed that independent advisors had more to offer the marketplace and the right business model for consumers. If we could help level the playing field, the business model would do the rest."

LPL Financial's services for independent advisors were slim at first. Advisors could pull customer records and download information, but the entire customer experience for the advisors was, as Stearns puts it, "not impressive." Advisors required software from other companies in addition to LPL Financial's in order to be fully effective.

"I realized that part of our job was going to be to connect people to the things they really needed in a more meaningful way," Stearns recalls. LPL Financial made a commitment to develop its own resources for independent advisors, creating "BranchNet," a proprietary web-based tool that provides services and information for advisors.

LPL Financial had to create a complete operational brokerage system. The commitment to BranchNet and the Internet meant that the firm's technology, banks of modems that allowed advisors dial-in access, would be phased out quickly. LPL Financial continued to develop BranchNet with scalability and efficiency in mind.

In 2000 the company began the process of creating a self-clearing capability, which would allow LPL Financial to take an order from an advisor and systematically complete the transaction of buying, selling, or redistributing the investors' assets. With this innovation, LPL Financial was able to give the wirehouses real competition.

> We LOOKED at the most HEAVILY USED products, received GOOD CUSTOMER FEEDBACK, and SHAPED THE CUSTOMER EXPERIENCE, examining things that WORKED and DIDN'T.

Stearns says, "After we built an operational brokerage system and a reporting system, it became a matter of interacting with customers about the use of their system. We looked at the most heavily-used products, received good customer feedback, and shaped the customer experience, examining what worked and what didn't work."

By 2005, the LPL Financial model was working so

well that advisors from the wirehouses were coming to LPL Financial in significant numbers. In 2005, two leading private equity firms, Hellman & Friedman LLC and Texas Pacific Group (TPG), became majority investors in LPL Financial. The transition from individual investor ownership to institutional investor ownership was another milestone for the company. This assured the company's ability to have the resources to continue to grow and compete on a large scale. That December, Mark Casady was tapped to run the company. Like Robinson, Casady is not a disciple of the Wall Street way. As Chairman and CEO, he wants to make sure advisors are happy and have growing businesses.

Today, independent advisors are connected in real time to all types of assets, people, products, and pricing. They can initiate, track, and report on a transaction at anytime through to completion. They have information to manage their client relationships and other tools. This includes consolidated LPL Financial account details, balances, positions, activity, cost basis, statements, and tax documents. Transactions are seamless. Advisors do not have to load anything onto their desktops or download data. Color printers and software enable advisors to display data and reports that are meaningful to their customers.

Stearns agrees that LPL Financial's priority is serving customers. "You can take our technology, but it is our people and our processes and the experience advisors have that is our business. It's hard to replicate."

Applause, please

There are tens of thousands of users accessing LPL Financial people, processes, and tools every day, including over 12,700 advisors and their staff. They do not hesitate to let the people at LPL Financial know what could be better.

How does LPL Financial continue to innovate a successful customer experience? Stearns explains, "We use our judgment, our staff's experience, and create a list of enhancements for our advisors. Then we go for the applause factor. At the conferences, we let them know about each thing on our list. We want to see which ones cause them to applaud most at the conference. That's what tells us."

Stearns notes, "The most important thing is, do they buy it? Do they pay every month for it, and if they don't, why not? These are entrepreneurs running tight ships and if they don't need it they are not going to pay for it. They will cancel their subscriptions." This attention to customers drives every new service and service enhancement at LPL Financial. In fact, it is part of every aspect of the firm's business, as reflected by the Commitment Creed—a pledge that sits on the desk of every employee, reminding them to put the customer first in everything they do.

Technology in the Background

The technology that allows LPL Financial to bring the resources of a major brokerage firm to an independent financial advisor is a critical part of what LPL Financial has developed. But the innovation has really been in how LPL Financial delivers the customer experience. Technology is in the background, and advisors choose LPL Financial for the way it helps them use that technology with their clients. It is easy to bring services, tools, and support to any remote office. Advisors can concentrate on building their businesses and accessing information for their clients, instead of putting valuable time into learning how to use the technology.

Stearns knows what it takes to keep the customer experience fresh and valuable. "Prior to LPL Financial, I came from a company where you created technology for other employees, and just gave it to them. We don't roll it out at LPL Financial like that. Our advisors can choose to buy or not to buy our tools and support. That means we have to make it very worthwhile for them and everyone who works with them."

LPL Financial has created an option for talented financial professionals who are also entrepreneurs. It has become a complete game changer for the industry.

In 2010, LPL Financial went public. In an interview with the *Wall Street Journal* in July 2009 about the "Rise of the Little Guy," Casady commented about Wall Street's meltdown and its upside for LPL Financial. "There's no doubt we're reaping the benefit of the destruction of trust by Wall Street." More and more brokers are moving from the traditional Wall Street powerhouse firms to LPL Financial, setting up their own independent financial advisories.

LPL FINANCIAL AT THE CROSSROAD

LPL Financial developed and delivered a new business paradigm that centered on the innovation of the customer experience and what the company's people, processes, technology, and services could do for customers. That customer experience gives LPL Financial the advantage, energizing and redefining the investment industry.

LPL Financial has not balked when reaching the crossroad of customer experience and technology. The company's goal has been to connect its customers to the services they need to run their own shops. As technology changes, LPL Financial adopts what works best for its customers and builds its services using the latest technological advances.

Chapter 7
Commit to the Customer Experience

"Our goal is to be earth's most customer-centric company."

—Jeff Bezos, Founder and CEO, Amazon

FOR MANY YEARS, ONE VISIONARY ENTREPRENEUR HAS been preaching the gospel of "customer experience." That man, Jeff Bezos, is the Founder, President, CEO, and Chairman of the Board of Amazon.com—the largest online retailer in the world. He has been on the front line of the customer experience revolution that has implications for every company that wants to create a solid foundation for future business.

Amazon has used three key strategies to build a premier customer experience. First, the company was willing to sacrifice short-term gains in order to build long-term value. Second, Amazon has used data to drive its customer experience. Third, the company continues to innovate with new ideas that move it closer to being the place to buy everything—books, electronics, music, clothing, household products...everything.

Today, Amazon is riding high, with a market

capitalization of over $100 billion, over 33,000 employees, and an ever-expanding empire of products sold over the Internet. But in 1995, this market dynamo was a start-up company with a leader who was learning on the job.

In an interview with the Academy of Achievement in 2001, Bezos recalled the early days at Amazon. "We were packing on our hands and knees on a hard concrete floor. I said to the person next to me, 'This packing is killing me! My back hurts, this is killing my knees on this hard cement floor.' I said, 'You know what we need? We need knee pads!' This person looked at me like I was the stupidest person they'd ever seen. 'What we need are packing tables.'"

Those humble beginnings when Amazon employees were up late packing boxes on the concrete floor helped create Amazon's culture of focus on the customer. Those early years forced them to galvanize the company culture around the customer experience.

Bezos founded Amazon.com in 1994 based on his recognition of the exponential growth in web usage at that time—2300 percent. He was working at a start-up company on Wall Street, building computer networks for brokers to clear trades. His idea to harness the business potential of Internet interest was to sell books online. He left Wall Street mid-year, forgoing his year-end bonus. In the same Academy of Achievement interview, Bezos notes, "When…you walk away from your annual bonus, that's the kind of thing that in the short-term can confuse you, but if you think about the long-term then you can really make good life decisions that you won't regret later." Bezos was committed for the long haul.

ESTABLISHING THE BRAND

Bezos was clear from the beginning that he had a long-range perspective for Amazon. In an interview with *Publishers Weekly* in 1998, he said, "Our strategy is not to make money. It's more important to spend significant money branding the site. We'll be in the harvest mode in the future." Amazon reported $81.7 million in sales in the first nine months of 1997 and lost $18.2 million. At that time, Amazon had 600 employees.

Amazon was launched in 1995 as an online seller of books. But Amazon customers were having such a good experience buying books that they asked to buy music, electronics, and other products. Amazon listened to its customers and expanded its operation. Music and DVDs were added in 1998. Electronics, toys, games, home improvement items, software, and video games came in 1999, less than four years after the company started.

FOCUS ON CUSTOMER EXPERIENCE PAYS OFF

In 2000, *Business Week Online* reported that Amazon's marketing cost to acquire a customer was less than any other e-tailer. At the same time, as Amazon added more products, each customer was buying more from year to year—from $106 annually in 1998 to $116 in 1999.

In 2002, seven years after its launch, Amazon finally showed a profit. By 2004 with $6.92 billion in sales, Amazon ranked at the top of *Internet Retailer's* annual top 400 list, well ahead of computer maker Dell, which posted $3.25 billion in online business-to-consumer sales that year. Office Depot, which has a partnership with Amazon, wasn't far behind with $3.1 billion that year. And in 2005, Amazon had nearly 49 million active customers who bought more electronics than books during that year's holiday blitz for the first time. Amazon had clearly defined itself as the leader of e-commerce by developing a company that was built to last.

Wall Street, however, has never placed much value in Mr. Bezos' emphasis on customers. What he viewed as money well spent—building customer loyalty—many investors saw as giving away money that should have gone to the bottom line. "What makes their core business so compelling is that they are focused on everything the customer wants," said Scott W. Devitt, who follows Amazon for Stifel Nicolaus & Company. "When you act in that manner many times Wall Street doesn't appreciate it." What Wall Street wanted from Amazon is what it always wants: short-term results. That is precisely what Dell tried to give investors when it scrimped on customer service and what eBay did when it heaped new costs on its most dedicated sellers. Eventually, these shortsighted decisions caught up with both companies. But Mr. Bezos refused to give in.

> **FOCUSING**
> on the CUSTOMER
> makes a
> COMPANY
> **MORE**
> **RESILIENT.**

According to *New York Times* columnist Joe Nocera, Amazon's "dogged pursuit of a better customer experience has turned out to be exactly right." By the end of 2007, Amazon customers were spending, on average, $184 a year. Forrester Research reported that 52 percent of people shopping online said they used Amazon to research products.

Making a company more resilient

The focus on customer experience paid off for Amazon. In a 2009 interview with Om Malik, Bezos explained, "Focusing on the customer makes a company more resilient." He purposely kept Amazon employees a key part of the process of creating the customer-centric company. Following the dot-com bust, he recognized that Amazon's business was continuing to grow. Bezos made the effort to communicate more with Amazon employees to ease their concern about the future of the company.

Bezos knows that a purchase is not made on price alone. When Amazon first started letting customers review books, some publishers were startled, because customers give both positive and negative reviews. Bezos knew that helping customers make an informed purchase decision creates *real* value. Making a bad purchase decision isn't just a waste of the money a customer has spent on the product, it's a waste of the customer's time spent with the product. Bezos was a pioneer in understanding that the balance of power was shifting from the company to the customer, and the customer was controlling the conversation.

> Bezos's philosophy **is that** A COMPANY is **NOT** defined BY ITS TECHNOLOGY, process, or PEOPLE, but by its **CUSTOMERS.**

Constantly Improving
THE CUSTOMER EXPERIENCE

In an interview with *Bloomberg Businessweek* in 2008, Bezos addressed Amazon's continuation to innovate whether times are good or bad. "I'm not sure we have a choice," said Bezos. He is determined to avoid the common business pitfall of making business decisions based on the company's skill set rather than on the customers' needs and desires. "That approach puts a finite lifetime on a company, because the world changes and what used to be cutting-edge skills have turned into something your customers may not need anymore." Bezos's strategy has been to determine what the customers want, and then go find people who have the skills to deliver those products and services. Bezos's philosophy is that a company is not defined by its technology, process, or people, but by its customers.

Shareowners' Interests Aligned
WITH CUSTOMERS' INTERESTS

In 2011, Amazon continues to invest heavily in innovation for the benefit of the customer experience. But Bezos finally has shareholders convinced of the power of customer experience. "We have unshakeable conviction that the long-term interests of shareowners are perfectly aligned with the interests of customers," he wrote in a letter to shareholders in April 2011. "Invention is in our DNA and technology is the fundamental tool we wield to evolve and improve every aspect of the experience we provide our customers." Despite Amazon's report of first-quarter profit dropping 33 percent, the stock price held steady and even increased.

The growth of the Amazon marketplace did not happen overnight. It evolved over time. Consistently and consciously, Amazon perfected its technology, sold merchants on the concept, overcame objections, and integrated the platform.

CX IN THE COMPANY DNA

Gary Tucker, Senior Vice President at J.D. Power and Associates, says that companies like Amazon "pay very close attention to culture. If we were going to make a macro observation as to companies that 'get it' and those that don't, it is about the culture of that company from the top down that prioritizes the customer experience." At these companies, customer experience isn't a responsibility assigned to one department or executive. Customer experience is the responsibility of the whole company, and is led by the CEO.

Companies that provide extraordinary experiences have customer advocacy embedded deep in their company culture. And it didn't get there by accident. They work on it every day. They don't necessarily get it right the first time—or the second time—or the third—but it is always a company priority. Continuous focus assures that they get there. The great ones also guard against complacency. A company must make this a commitment to be successful at delivering great experiences to its customers.

Designing great experiences must be in the companies' DNA. At Intuit, creating and delivering great experiences as a differentiator or margin protector is not even the focus. They create great experiences because it is the right thing to do. And every employee knows this. Phil Ohme, Principal Interaction Designer at Intuit, explains, "If something is not going to make a task or a job easier for the end consumer, then we don't need to be doing it." Intuit seeks to change its customers' financial lives so profoundly that they cannot imagine going back to the old way.

CEO AS CUSTOMER EXPERIENCE ADVOCATE

Tucker at J.D. Power notes that customer experience focus "has to start with the leadership—it always starts at the top." Steve Jobs at Apple, Scott Cook at Intuit, and Jeff Bezos at Amazon—they have all been the Chief CX Advocate or the Chief "Evangelist" for determining, developing, and delivering the experience. Larry Tesler, discusses what it was like working directly with Steve Jobs when Tesler was Vice President and Chief Scientist at Apple Computer: "You could show him that X was a better design than Y and despite all of the issues that people would come back to you with about schedules and engineering limitations and prices and whatever, he would just cut through it and make a decision, taking into account the users' experience more than anything. Whether it was positioning in the marketing message, or customer service and support, or upgrades and repairs, Steve Jobs usually said, 'delay the product so you can fix it.'" Jobs was not afraid to delay a product launch date at

> When the **CEO** has a **PASSION** for the **CUSTOMER EXPERIENCE**, IT CAN GET INTO THE **DNA** of the **COMPANY.**

Apple to ensure that the customer experience was right.

Tesler makes a similar comment when discussing his time working alongside Jeff Bezos at Amazon. "Amazon's success is Jeff Bezos, in terms of the success of user experience." Bezos as the number one customer advocate at Amazon is the reason why the company is so successful, according to Tesler, who was Amazon's VP of Shopping Experience. Bezos learned very early on that Amazon's customer experience was the most important factor in its success. He made customer experience a priority from the start. Bezos made it a point to do everything he could to learn about the customer—talk with the customer support people, watch customers, study the A/B test results, attend usability sessions, read emails from customers—to ensure that Amazon paid attention to customers and really understood their needs.

It starts with the CEO. When the CEO has a passion for the customer experience, it can get into the DNA of the company. Kaaren Hanson, Intuit's Vice President of Design Innovation, says that at Intuit, the CEO starts meetings with his general managers by going on customer visits first. According to Hanson, "Our CEO spends many hours out with customers, partly because he wants to stay in touch with customers and partly because he is modeling the behavior that he expects from everyone on his team and throughout the organization."

Old school thinking—"we have always done it this way"—is a trap. Old-school thinking—"we are making money on our product now, why would we want to change anything?"—will not carry you into the rapidly changing future. Complacency in your market will cost you. You must adapt quickly in the customer experience economy.

Chapter 8
The CX Revolution: Who's Next?

"It was clear to us that cost reductions and improved operating efficiencies alone were not enough. True transformation would require us to improve our customer experience."

—HOWARD SCHULTZ, CHAIRMAN, PRESIDENT, AND CEO OF STARBUCKS

THE CUSTOMER EXPERIENCE JOURNEY STARTS WHEN A prospect, customer or advocate *first* interacts in any way with a company. That interaction can be direct—the company's advertising or actual experience using a product or service. It can also be indirect through many influencers—reviews, articles, research, word-of-mouth, or social networking.

Creating a company that focuses on the customer experience takes exceptional commitment from everyone in the company. Moving a business beyond promises, products, services, pricing, and transactions is not an experiment, a project, or the domain of one department.

Companies that understand the value of exceptional customer experience start with a vision of what the customer experience should be. The vision is based on in-depth knowledge of the customer and the product or service.

Successful customer experience companies sometimes

> **Companies that UNDERSTAND THE VALUE OF EXCEPTIONAL customer experience start WITH A VISION of what the CUSTOMER EXPERIENCE should be.**

falter or fail along the way. But when they have faltered, they have regrouped by focusing on the rejuvenation of valuable experiences for customers. They determine again what the experience should be, then develop it with and for the customers. They deliver the product or service anew with an experience so extraordinary that it changes potential customers to customers, and loyal customers to energized advocates.

Anticipating the Customer Experience Lifecycle

We call the people at companies who deliver exceptional customer experiences "experience makers." During our interviews for this book with experience makers at various companies, many spoke about the surprises they had and what they learned along the way when developing a great customer experience. These experience makers use their interaction with customers to help guide their decision-making, but they can also anticipate what the customer wants, even before the customer asks for it.

The ability of experience makers to anticipate the next generation of the customer experience lifecycle is based on their experience, business performance success, and a thorough connectedness with people. This creates a contextual bridge to successfully anticipate what could be next. Steve Jobs talked about anticipating customers' desires in a 2000 article in *Fortune*. "This is what customers pay us for—to sweat all these details so it's easy and pleasant for them to use our computers. We're supposed to be really good at this. That doesn't mean we don't listen to customers, but it's hard for them to tell you what they want when they've never seen anything remotely like it. Take desktop video editing. I never got one request from someone who wanted to edit movies on his computer. Yet now that people see it, they say, 'Oh my God, that's great!'"

How the experience makers think

Large or small, experience makers think long term. They are not looking to flip a company for quick profit.

Experience makers start with an understanding of what the customer experience is now—a baseline. Then they determine specifically what the customer experience *should* be. Experience makers do not constrain themselves by old school thinking, a single industry, or by markets or technologies. Experience makers are, for now, uncommon, but they are found in a growing group of companies. Their businesses are defined by what they Do-For customers, not by what their products or services do.

When experience makers look at an opportunity, they evaluate the quality of the experience customers are having both with their competitors and even outside their own industry. A great customer experience, wherever it is found, raises customers' expectations for great customer experiences everywhere.

YOUR TOUGHEST COMPETITOR SHOULD BE YOU

At their best, experience makers vigorously compete with themselves. They know the answer to the question: Are we there yet? It is generally "no." They know that leading the market with the best customer experience is a brief stop along the way to innovating the next experience. Even if they are out front with large market share, above average profit margins, and customers advocating enthusiastically, they constantly reinvigorate and innovate the customer experience.

METRICS OF SUCCESS ARE ALIGNED WITH DELIVERING EXTRAORDINARY EXPERIENCES

In companies that care about the customer experience, internal measures are put in place to ensure that improvement of the customer experience will lead to company success.

Dell Computer was one of the earliest companies to include the term "Customer Experience" in position titles. In an article in *Fast Company* in 1999, writer Scott Kirstner noted that "nearly every bulletin board in every office has a sign that reads 'The Customer Experience: Own It'." As part of its turnaround, Dell changed its metrics of success for customer service phone representatives from the goal of pure internal efficiency to the goal of customer problem resolution. That kind of customer focus showed how Dell took its bulletin-board mantra to heart.

THE CUSTOMER EXPERIENCE HIERARCHY

The Customer Experience Hierarchy shows the stages of a company's development of its customer experience. Most companies today are in Stages 1 and 2. Very few are at the top of the hierarchy. The hierarchy follows a company's growth path as it moves from start-up to established and successful, as it relates to the importance of building a great customer experience.

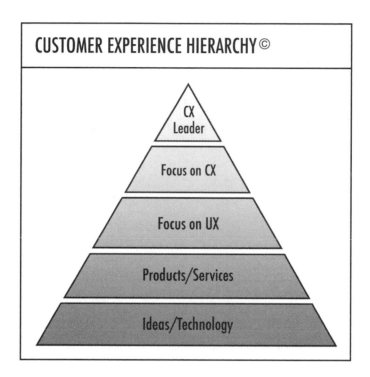

CUSTOMER EXPERIENCE HIERARCHY©

CX Leader

Focus on CX

Focus on UX

Products/Services

Ideas/Technology

Stage 1: Ideas/Technology

Companies start with ideas, technology or both. People commit to their ideas and move forward with other people, resources, processes, and messages to build the business.

Stage 2: Products and Services

The company develops its products or services. Competition in the market is based on the product's or service's features or benefits.

Stage 3: Focus on User Experience (UX)

The company develops a pleasing user experience for its products or services. That user experience recognizes what the product or service will Do-For the customer.

Stage 4: Development of a True Customer Experience (CX)

When the company recognizes that the customer experience is much broader than the end-user interaction, it makes a long-term commitment to assure most interactions people have with the company are positive. They determine, develop, and deliver a customer experience that is better, different, and more valuable than the competition's.

Stage 5: Customer Experience Leadership

The company is committed to assuring that all interactions with their messages, people, processes, products, or services are pleasing. It delights people at every step of the customer experience: intriguing them as potential customers, satisfying them when they buy, and continuing to outperform until their customers become advocates. The company transforms its market and changes peoples' lives for the better. From the CEO down, everyone at the company is committed to retaining the customer experience leadership position.

Gary Tucker of J.D. Power and Associates defines the

Stage 5 companies: "Those who really understand the customer experience, its value as a competitive advantage and their desire to get better."

CUSTOMER EXPERIENCE TWELVE ESSENTIALS

Companies at stages 4 and 5 on the Customer Experience Hierarchy follow what we call the "Twelve Essentials of Customer Experience." These are the elements we have identified that are key to building a company focused on delivering great customer experience.

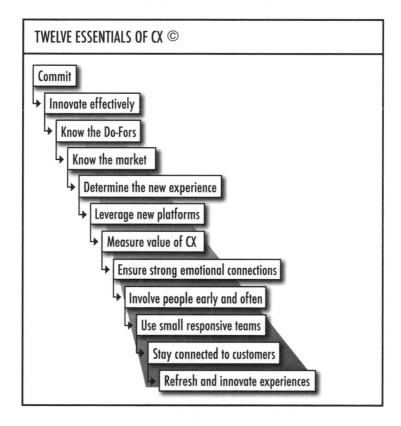

TWELVE ESSENTIALS OF CX ©

- Commit
- Innovate effectively
- Know the Do-Fors
- Know the market
- Determine the new experience
- Leverage new platforms
- Measure value of CX
- Ensure strong emotional connections
- Involve people early and often
- Use small responsive teams
- Stay connected to customers
- Refresh and innovate experiences

1. **Commitment from the CEO.**

   The companies with the best customer experiences typically have commitment from the top—the CEO, founder, or business owner. Setting the direction for the company is key to developing a customer-centric business.

2. **Innovation and new ideas drive great customer experience.**

   Companies need to understand how to use innovation to determine, develop, and deliver great customer experiences.

3. **Know the Do-Fors of your product or service.**

   A company must understand what customers want the product or service to Do-For them. Then the customer experience is built around the customers' needs, not the company's.

4. **Know the market.**

   Look at the customer experience for all segments of the market—potential customers, current customers, and advocates. Benchmark those experiences for the major competitors in the market.

5. **Purposely design the customer experience.**

   The best customer experiences are specific, and those companies know exactly how their experiences are better, different, and more valuable for customers. It is important for a company to be realistic about what it can promise and deliver.

6. **Incorporate new communications platforms into the customer experience.**

    Customers' preferences change. A company must decide which changes will keep it relevant, create new business opportunities, or expand the reach. Customer experiences across different communications platforms must be a consistent extension of the great overall customer experience of the company. Social technologies and new communications platforms need to do something for the company, not to the company.

7. **Measure the value of the customer experience.**

    Independent researchers like J.D. Power, Forrester, Gartner, and others measure the value that customer experience adds to a business. Metrics of success should be aligned with delivering extraordinary customer experiences, along with other business goals.

8. **Use customer experience to create an emotional connection.**

    Developing an emotional connection with the customer helps to create trust in the product and the company.

9. **Involve customers when determining and developing the customer experience.**

   Ask, watch, and listen to customers—early and often—when it will be less expensive and easier to make changes, for the biggest return and impact.

10. **Small teams work best to develop new ideas.**

    Smaller teams of eight people or less are easier to manage and make communication simpler. When prototypes are simple, it is easier to do rapid iterations of changes, increasing their complexity as testing shows their success.

11. **Stay connected to customers—not processes**

    When a company reaches a crossroad, it is important to stay connected to the customers. Leave behind methods, equipment, processes, and technologies that might separate the company from customers and future opportunities.

12. **Continuously reinvigorate existing customer experiences and innovate new experiences.**

    The best customer experience companies compete with themselves so that they continue to improve.

THE CUSTOMER EXPERIENCE REVOLUTION

A quick search on Monster.com yields over 1,000 job positions with the keywords "Customer Experience." The range of companies represented includes several we would expect to see: Intuit, Apple, Amazon. But the companies listed also include banks, retail clothing stores, healthcare providers, insurance companies, cable service providers, restaurants, and many others. Some are thinly disguised customer service positions, but more and more often, companies have established a true Customer Experience function and are staffing that department with employees whose responsibilities include creating and maintaining exceptional customer experiences.

On October 1, 2011, Paul Copses began his new job as General Motors' very first U.S. Vice President of Customer Experience. According to GM's press release, he reports to GM North America President Mark Reuss and "regularly updates" GM Chairman and CEO Dan Akerson. Such a highly-placed position in a major company reveals the powerful influence of the concept of customer experience among the top echelon of established corporate America.

The momentum of the customer experience revolution is building. Industries will be transformed by companies that embrace the concept of great customer experience.

New players are entering the customer experience arena. Their success will depend on their ability to determine what the customer experience should be, and their long-term commitment to creating that experience.

The Customer Experience Revolution is here!

Bibliography

Albanesius, Chloe. "Sony, Kodak: Personal Camcorders Will Survive Flip's Demise," *PCMag*, April 15, 2011, http://www.pcmag.com/article2/0,2817,2383636,00.asp#fbid=0dbBDEI9YPC.

"Amazon: E-Commerce Success Story," *CBSNews Tech* (blog), *CBSNews.com*, February 11, 2009, http://www.cbsnews.com/stories/2005/07/05/tech/main706351.shtml.

Arguin, Claudel. *Emotional Durability Is the New Sustainability: Why Are Objects Cherished Even after Their Functionality Has Been Surpassed* (thesis), Northumbria University, U.K., 2010.

"Bezos On Innovation" (interview), *Bloomberg Businessweek*, April 17, 2008, http://www.businessweek.com/magazine/content/08_17/b4081064880218.htm.

Bigelow, Bruce. "San Diego's EMN8 Raises $14.4M for Self-Service Sales Kiosks," Xconomy, March 16, 2010, http://www.xconomy.com/san-diego/2010/03/16/san-diegos-emn8-raises-14-4m-for-self-service-sales-kiosks.

Blockbuster Annual Report, 1999.

Burkett, Grady. Morningstar Analyst Report, February 17, 2011.

Burkett, Grady. Morningstar Analyst Report, May 6, 2011.

Burns, Megan, with Harley Manning and Jennifer Peterson. "The Customer Experience Index, 2011," (report), January 11, 2011, http://forrester.com/rb/Research/customer_experience_index,_2011/q/id/58251/t/2.

Burrows, Peter. "Stephen Elop's Nokia Adventure," *Bloomberg Businessweek*, June 2, 2011, http://www.businessweek.com/magazine/content/11_24/b4232056703101.htm.

Business Exchange, "ComplianceMax Financial Corporation" (IT Services entry), *Bloomberg Businessweek*, http://www.xconomy.com/san-diego/2010/03/16/san-diegos-emn8-raises-14-4m-for-self-service-sales-kiosks.

Capps, Robert. "The Good Enough Revolution: When Cheap and Simple Is Just Fine," *Wired*, August 24, 2009, http://www.wired.com/gadgets/miscellaneous/magazine/17-09/ff_goodenough.

"Cisco Public Corporate Overview," Cisco.com, http://newsroom.cisco.com/documents/10157/1204766/Public_Corporate_Overview_FY11_Q3.pdf.

Corty, Michael. "Netflix's Letter to Customers Is a Panic Move," Morningstar Analyst Note, September 19, 2011.

Emeran, Riyad. "Apple iPhone Review," *Trusted Reviews* (blog), November 8, 2007, http://www.trustedreviews.com/mobile-phones/review/2007/11/08/Apple-iPhone/p1.

"EMN8 Named Finalist for 2010 Red Herring 100 North America Award," *PRWeb*, June 22, 2010, http://www.prweb.com/releases/2010/EMN8RedHerringFinalist/prweb4174034.htm.

"Entrepreneurial Leaders from Pure Digital Technologies, Inc., Accretive Health, Inc., and LogMeIn, Inc. Receive Ernst & Young's 2010 Venture Capital Award of Excellence," *PR Newswire*, November 15, 2010, http://www.prnewswire.com/news-releases/entrepreneurial-leaders-from-pure-digital-technologies-inc-accretive-health-inc-and-logmein-inc-receive-ernst--youngs-2010-venture-capital-award-of-excellence-108171619.html.

"First Online DVD Rental Store Opens" (press release), Netflix. com, April 14, 1998, http://netflix.mediaroom.com/index. php?s=43&item=232.

Fritz, Ben. "Once High-Flying Netflix Is Now Stumbling," *Los Angeles Times*, September 19, 2011, http://articles.latimes.com/2011/ sep/19/business/la-fi-ct-netflix-20110920.

Garrahan, Matthew. "Amazon Launches Web Film Service," *FT.com*, February 23, 2011, http://www.ft.com/intl/cms/s/0/a9c43324-3ed8-11e0-834e-00144feabdc0.html#axzz1dhiKZ14h.

Garrahan, Matthew. "Walmart Rises in Digital Battle." *FT.com*, February 6, 2011 http://www.ft.com/intl/cms/s/0/ec2fe9ba-3230-11e0-a820-00144feabdc0.html#axzz1dhiKZ14h.

Gina. "Sony Talks! About the MP4 Camera Market," The Sony Blog (blog), April 14, 2011, http://blog.sony.com/sony-talks-about-the-mp4-camera-market.

"GM Appoints U.S. Vice President, Customer Experience" (GM press release), GM.com, September 27, 2011, http://media. gm.com/content/media/us/en/gm/news.detail.html/content/ Pages/news/us/en/2011/Sep/0927_copsesvp.

Gobe, Marc. *Emotional Branding: The New Paradigm for Connecting Brands to People*, New York: Allworth Press, 2001.

Goldman, Joshua. "Flip Alternatives Worth Buying – And a Couple to Skip," *Crave* (blog), *CNET*, April 15, 2011, http://news.cnet. com/8301-17938_105-20054282-1.html.

"Great Minds of Business: Howard Schultz," (video), History.com, http://www.history.com/videos/great-minds-of-business-howard-schultz#great-minds-of-business-howard-schultz.

Guiste, Matthew. "Open Innovation and Social Media" (video), Leaderlab.com, http://www.youtube.com/watch?v=pjNM8drAqG0.

Hansen, Randy. "Camcorder Buyer's Guide 2006," Videomaker, December 2006, http://www.videomaker.com/article/12656/2.

Ignelzi, R.J. "Personal Shoppers Give the Royal Treatment — For Free," *San Diego Union-Tribune*, January 16, 2011, http://www.signonsandiego.com/news/2011/jan/16/the-royal-treatment-for-free.

"Intuit to Acquire Mint.com" (press release), Mint.com, September 14, 2009, https://www.mint.com/press/intuit-to-acquire-mint-com.

"Inventing E-Commerce" (interview with Jeff Bezos), Academy of Achievement website, http://www.achievement.org/autodoc/page/bez0int-3.

J.D. Power and Associates, "2011 U.S. Full Service Investor Satisfaction Study," (report), June 2011.

J.D. Power and Associates, "Achieving Excellence in Customer Service" (report), February 2011.

Jarvis, Jeff. "Dell Learns to Listen," *Bloomberg Businessweek*, October 17, 2007, http://www.businessweek.com/bwdaily/dnflash/content/oct2007/db20071017_277576.htm.

Jobs, Steve. "Apple's One-Dollar-a-Year Man," *Fortune*, January 24, 2000, http://money.cnn.com/magazines/fortune/fortune_archive/2000/01/24/272277.

Keane, Robert. "Making the Future Happen," *Investment Advisor*, May 2006, http://www.advisorone.com/2006/05/01/making-the-future-happen.

Kim, Ryan. "Flip SlideHD Camcorder Helps Users View Videos," SFGate.com, April 13, 2010, http://articles.sfgate.com/2010-04-13/business/20846913_1_pure-digital-technologies-new-flip-video.

"Kiosks Come to Jack in the Box," QSR, June 4, 2009, http://www.qsrmagazine.com/news/kiosks-come-jack-box.

Kirstner, Scott. "The Customer Experience," *Fast Company*, September 30, 1999, http://www.fastcompany.com/magazine/nc01/012.html.

BIBLIOGRAPHY

MacMillan, Douglas. "Turning Smartphones Into Cash registers," *Bloomberg Businessweek*, February 14, 2011.

Malik, Om. "Tips on Innovation & Entrepreneurship From Jeff Bezos," *Gigaom.com*, June 15, 2009, http://gigaom.com/2009/06/15/tips-on-innovation-enterprenuership-from-jeff-bezos.

McCarty, Dawn, Linda Sander, and Tiffany Kary. "Blockbuster Files for Bankruptcy after Online Rivals Gain," *Bloomberg Businessweek*, September 23, 2010, http://www.bloomberg.com/news/2010-09-23/blockbuster-video-rental-chain-files-for-bankruptcy-protection.html.

Morningstar Analysis Report, Starbucks Corporation, April 28, 2011.

Morrison, Scott. Amazon's Bezos Says Investments Will Pay Off," *MarketWatch* (blog), *Wall Street Journal*, April 27, 2011, http://www.marketwatch.com/story/amazons-bezos-says-investments-will-pay-off-2011-04-27.

Netflix Annual Report, 2002.

Netflix Annual Report, 2010.

"Netflix Passes 10 Million Subscribers, With 600,000 Net Additions Since the First of the Year" (press release), Netflix.com, February 12, 2009, http://netflix.mediaroom.com/index.php?s=43&item=307.

"Netflix to Offer New Unlimited DVD Plans and Will Separate Streaming and DVD Plans in the U.S." (press release), Netflix.com, July 12, 2011, http://netflix.mediaroom.com/index.php?s=43&item=397.

Nocera, Joe. "Put Buyers First? What a Concept," *Technology* (blog), *New York Times*, January 5, 2008, http://www.nytimes.com/2008/01/05/technology/05nocera.html?ex=1357275600&en=3b6e9e83e0180d5d&ei=5124&partner=permalink&exprod=permalink.

Norman, Donald. *Emotional Design: Why We Love (or Hate) Everyday Things,* New York: Basic Books, 2003.

Picoult, Jon. "Yes, Virginia, There Is a Return on Customer Experience Investments," *Customer Think* (blog), February 6, 2010, http://www.customerthink.com/article/return_on_customer_experience_investments.

Pine II, B. Joseph and James H. Gilmore. *The Experience Economy: Work Is Theater & Every Business a Stage*, Boston: Harvard Business Press, 1999.

Poggi, Jay. "The Rise and Fall of Blockbuster," *Newsweek*, September 23, 2010.

Pogue, David. "The iPhone Matches Most of Its Hype," *Circuits* (blog), *New York Times*, June 27, 2007, http://www.nytimes.com/2007/06/27/technology/circuits/27pogue.html.

Pogue, David. "The Tragic Death of the Flip," *Pogue's Posts* (blog), *New York Times*, April 14, 2011, http://pogue.blogs.nytimes.com/2011/04/14/the-tragic-death-of-the-flip.

Reid, Calvin. "Amazon.com's Jeff Bezos: Brand First, Profits Come Later*,*" *Publishers Weekly*, January 5, 1998, http://www.publishersweekly.com/pw/by-topic/industry-news/bookselling/article/45954-amazon-com-s-jeff-bezos-brand-first-profits-come-later.html.

Schorn, Daniel. "The Brain Behind Netflix," *60 Minutes*, February 11, 2009, http://www.cbsnews.com/stories/2006/12/01/60minutes/main2222059.shtml.

Schultz, Howard with Joanne Gordon. *Onward: How Starbucks Fought for Its life Without Losing Its Soul*, New York: Rodale Press, 2011.

Shambra, Jessica. "Consumers Flip for Mini Camcorders," *Fortune Tech Daily*, January 27, 2009, http://money.cnn.com/2009/01/27/technology/flip_cams.fortune/index.htm.

Smith, Randall. "The Rise of the Little Guy," *Wall Street Journal*, July 3, 2009, http://online.wsj.com/article/SB124657902506589439.html.

Spector, Mike and Joseph Checkler. "Dish Network Wins

Blockbuster," *Wall Street Journal*, April 7, 2011, http://online.
wsj.com/article/SB1000142405274870410160457624601 3124
028834.html.

Starbucks Corporation Annual Reports, 2000 – 2010.

"Suddenly, Amazon's Books Look Better," *Bloomberg Businessweek*,
February 21, 2000, http://www.businessweek.com/2000/00_08/
b3669091.htm.

Summers, Nick. "A Straight Shooter," *Newsweek*, September 20, 2010.

Swisher, Kara. "Pure Digital's Jonathan Kaplan–aka the Flip Guy–
Speaks (Post-Cisco)!" All Things D, April 6, 2009, http://
allthingsd.com/20090406/pure-digitals-jonathan-kaplan-aka-
the-flip-guy-speaks-post-cisco.

Taylor, Suzanne and Kathy Schroeder. *Inside Intuit: How the Makers
of Quicken Beat Microsoft and Revolutionized an Entire Industry*,
Boston: Harvard Business Press, 2003.

Temkin, Bruce. "The State of Customer Experience Management,
2011" (report), May 2011.

Temkin, Bruce, with Moira Dorsey, William Chu, and Angela Beckers.
"Customer Experience Boosts Revenue" (report), June 22, 2009.

"The Crucial Mission: Provide Customers with What They Want,"
Bloomberg Businessweek E-Biz (website), March 16, 1999, http://
www.businessweek.com/ebiz/9903/316bezos.htm.

"US Patent Issued to Cisco Technology on Feb. 22 for "Digital
Video Camera with Retractable Data Connector and Resident
Software Application" (California Inventors)," High Beam
Research, February 24, 2011, http://www.highbeam.com/
doc/1P3-2275176501.html.

Vance, Ashlee. "A Tiny Camcorder Has a Big Payday," *New York
Times*, March 20, 2009.

Van Tyne, Sean. "Corporate UX Maturity: A Model for
Organizations," *User Experience*, Vol. 9, Issue 1, 2010.

Wakabayashi, Daisuke and Christopher Lawton. "Sony Turns Focus to Low-Cost Video Camera," *Wall Street Journal*, April 16, 2009, http://online.wsj.com/article/SB123983131210022415.html.

Witt, Larry. "As the King of Search, Google Enjoys an Enviable Position," Morningstar Equity Research, January 20, 2011.

Index

INDEX